PRACTICAL ELECTRONIC
PROJECT BUILDING

PRACTICAL ELECTRONIC PROJECT BUILDING

ALAN C AINSLIE

Edited by
MORRIS A COLWELL

NEWNES TECHNICAL BOOKS

THE BUTTERWORTH GROUP

UNITED KINGDOM
Butterworth & Co (Publishers) Ltd
London: 88 Kingsway, WC2B 6AB

AUSTRALIA
Butterworths Pty Ltd
Sydney: 586 Pacific Highway, Chatswood, NSW 2067
Also at Melbourne, Brisbane, Adelaide
and Perth

CANADA
Butterworth & Co (Canada) Ltd
Toronto: 2265 Midland Avenue, Scarborough, Ontario M1P 4S1

NEW ZEALAND
Butterworths of New Zealand Ltd
Wellington: 26—28 Waring Taylor Street, 1

SOUTH AFRICA
Butterworth & Co (South Africa) (Pty) Ltd
Durban: 152—154 Gale Street

USA
Butterworth (Publishers) Inc
Boston: 19 Cummings Park, Woburn, Mass. 01801

First published in 1976 by Newnes Technical Books

A Butterworth imprint

© Butterworth & Co (Publishers) Ltd, 1976

ISBN 0 408 00231 X

Typeset by Butterworths LPD
Printed and bound in England by The Pitman Press, Bath

PREFACE

Probably the most rewarding aspect of electronics, either as a hobby or professionally, is the achievement of making up a project and seeing it working. The present day constructor has a choice of construction methods, each of which merits attention. To provide a comprehensive manual on all construction techniques would be more than the average constructor needs to make a working prototype. This book presents a concise but informative guide to some of the current popular methods usually employed. Some hints are also given on finishing and basic fault-finding methods.

Newcomers to electronics will find many useful hints; it is recommended that further reference is also made to magazines which regularly provide a service of constructional project designs to build. This book has been prepared with the aim of complementing the details given in published projects. It can be kept close to hand where construction work is carried out so that reference can be made when required.

Additional guidance on various other aspects of constructional work are provided in companion volumes in this series of Constructor's Guides. For the more adventurous, *Project Planning and Building* provides more detailed information on some of the techniques shown here. Further general data and tables will also be found in other Constructor's Guides.

In preparing a book of this kind it has been necessary to include a selection of illustrations showing the methods described. The author is particularly grateful to have had the help of many firms in supplying materials and equipment to do this, and to all of them (listed on the next page) and particularly to Rankolor Laboratories, Mansfield, he expresses his sincere thanks, without whose help the presentation would not have been the same.

Morris A. Colwell

ACKNOWLEDGMENTS

The author wishes to express his gratitude to the following Companies who have kindly assisted in the preparation of this book.

Adcola Products Ltd.
Amtron (UK) Ltd.
Antex Electronics Ltd.
Arbour Electronics Ltd.
P. T. Barclay and Partners Ltd.
Black & Decker Ltd.
W. H. Brady Co. Ltd.
Chartpak Ltd.
Chinaglia (UK) Ltd.
Circuitape Ltd.
Circuit-stik Inc. (USA)
Combined Electronic Services Ltd.
Data Publications Ltd.
Decon Laboratories Ltd.
Doram Electronics Ltd.
Douglas Electronic Industries Ltd.
Eddystone Radio Ltd.
Eraser International Ltd.
Finnigans Speciality Paints Ltd.
Greenwood Electronics
Guest Electronic Distribution Ltd.
Heath (Gloucester) Ltd.
H. M. Electronics
Humbrol Ltd.
I.C.I. Ltd. Plastics Division

Josty (UK) Ltd.
Kodak Ltd.
Letraset (UK) Ltd.
Linton Laboratories Ltd.
G. F. Milward Ltd.
Mullard Ltd.
Multicore Solders Ltd.
E. R. Nicholls
Nombrex (1969) Ltd.
P. C. Services (Proto Components)
Pentel (Stationery) Ltd.
Philips Electrical Ltd.
Precision Electronic Terminations
    (EMI) Ltd.
Ramar Constructor Services Ltd.
Rastra Electronics Ltd.
Redpoint Ltd.
Scopex Instruments Ltd.
Sinclair Radionics Ltd.
J. E. Sugden & Co. Ltd.
Thomas Haddon & Stokes Ltd.
Thorn Lighting Ltd.
Tuckers (Sheffield) Ltd.
Vero Electronics Ltd.
Weller Electric Ltd.
West Hyde Developments Ltd.

CONTENTS

1 Tools and basic skills

Since electronics is classed as a light industry, it comes within the scope of almost any enthusiastic amateur, who can reap tremendous rewards and self-satisfaction from his creative achievements. Elaborate equipment is not really needed and difficult metalwork can be avoided by taking advantage of the availability of so many well-designed commercial cases and cabinets. Electronics construction work need not be at all messy and requires little space to be 'borrowed' from the household for a 'workshop'.

A complete project can easily be bundled into a box for storage so nothing really permanent is required—in the early stages at least. The domestic table-top suits the purpose admirably; kitchen or boxroom space is often free for long periods in the evenings, and should be reasonably comfortable and particularly well lit.

Lighting is an important point as poor lighting (including bright lighting that causes one to work in one's own shadow) can lead to eye strain and fatigue. Fluorescent lighting is generally good as it forms only faint shadows and is of the right colour to enable component colour codes to be read without difficulty. Tungsten filament lamps tend to be rather yellow and can present difficulties when trying to distinguish blue from violet.

To protect the surface of the table from scratches and solder burns a piece of plywood faced with white Formica can be used as a bench top. In setting out to start project building it is important to position the soldering iron correctly. A right-handed person uses his right hand to solder, therefore, the mains lead drifts about the right-hand side of the bench. Thus the project under construction and all small parts should be kept well clear of this area. It is recommended that a safety guard or stand is used for the soldering iron on the right hand side,

1

together with the relatively heavy hand tools which are not disturbed by the iron mains lead and are conveniently to hand. Test equipment is best placed at the back or left-hand side of the bench.

A collection of tobacco tins is useful for keeping small components in, such as resistors and screws, otherwise these easily roll away. It sometimes helps to identify the various components for a project before work commences so that they are readily to hand. This reduces errors if one is not used to colour codes. The components can be stuck in a piece of expanded polystyrene with the value written by the side, or even attached to the project component list.

The number of tools that are required basically to start construction is surprisingly small. A basic kit, covering electronic assembly but not metalwork, would probably be:

Soldering iron, wire cutters, miniature long-nose pliers, small screwdrivers with both flat and crosshead blades.

For most work a 15 W soldering iron should suffice—its advantages being the small tip size. For regular work using tag strips, however, a

Small hand tools for electronics construction. From left to right: Long-nosed wiring pliers; Flat-end wire nippers; Diagonal or side cutters; Flat-nosed wiring pliers. All have insulated handles

25 W iron would be a better proposition. The constructor may prefer to compromise by using a thermostatic or temperature controlled iron—now on the market at quite reasonable prices. These are available with large and very small tips and have the heat retaining capacity for the large joint without overheating fine connections on printed circuit boards. With these irons it is very difficult to spoil a joint.

2

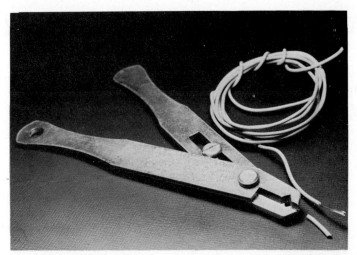

Bib wire strippers with adjustable blade aperture; can also be used for cutting wires

The tip of an iron is usually earthed for safety but to prevent leakage currents damaging components an isolated tip is recommended. The fact that the iron is earthed must be remembered when working on live circuitry—a practice not to be recommended.

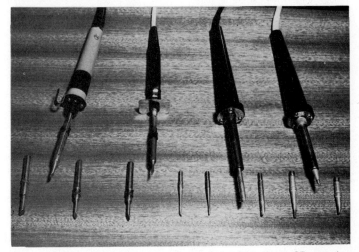

Soldering irons for electronics construction. Left to right: Antex 25 watt; Antex 15W low leakage iron with ceramic stem (Type CCN); Weller 25W standard; Weller TCP1 thermostatic iron

Low voltage irons are blessed with much lower leakage than those running directly from the mains but do need a low voltage power supply. A mains voltage iron of very low leakage is the Antex CCN series. These irons use a ceramic insulated tip to reduce leakage to such a low level that even CMOS (a very delicate logic i.c. family) can be soldered without special precautions.

Wire cutters can take many forms and may be in combination with wire strippers. Although the 'nipper' type of cutter is extensively used, it is worth noting that the shock as the cutter 'snaps' through the wire after soldering to printed circuit boards can weaken soldered joints. Because of this the 'scissor' type of cutter is to be recommended for high reliability work.

Miniature pliers are an expensive but indispensable item for forming leads, holding nuts and retrieving small parts. They are also used as

This soldering iron operates independently of the mains from rechargeable batteries in the handle. The stand acts also as a charger. Leakage currents are zero (courtesy Greenwood Electronics)

heat shunts and to hold wires when soldering to prevent one's fingers getting burned.

A collection of small and medium screwdrivers (both normal and crosshead) is soon acquired by the constructor. A set of watchmaker's or jeweller's screwdrivers is very useful for intricate work.

There are several different types of crosshead screws in use but the two most common types are *Philips and *Pozidriv. The Philips head

* Registered Trade Marks

4

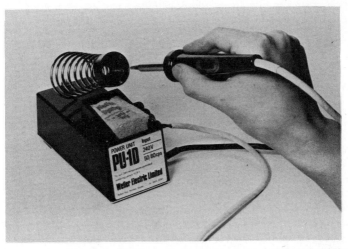

Low voltage iron the Weller TCP1 runs from a mains power unit in the stand. The damp sponge for cleaning is placed at the front of it. The temperature of operation depends on the tip that is fitted

requires a more pointed driver and using the wrong type can damage the screw. Japanese crosshead screws are easily loosened with a carefully used 'Pozidriv' type of screwdriver. Philips head screws are seldom made by most screw manufacturers.

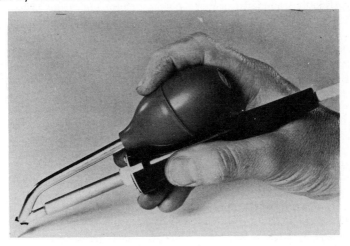

A suction desolder device attached to the TCP1 iron. The tip melts the solder and the rubber bulb is squeezed then released to draw up the solder

5

We shall see later how additional tools can be used to assist in various tasks but first let us look at the basic skill of construction work —soldering. (A good guide is 'The Soldering Handbook').

Soldering

The soldered joint forms the basic jointing method of all electronics work. A soldered joint is made between two metals by melting an alloy of lead and tin and making it 'flow' over the joined wires and/or other conductors. The soldering iron tool is heated to a temperature just a little higher than the melting point of the solder.

The tip of the iron is made of copper which has a high heat retaining capacity. The copper surface of the iron is 'tinned' as it first warms up from new by running clean solder over it and wiping quickly with a damp rag or sponge. This is necessary to prevent the tip oxidising and to promote solder flow.

With use the copper tip tends to be eroded by the resin core or flux in the solder, resulting in a small concave crater appearing in the tip; after a period of use the tip has to be filed smooth again and retinned. This wasteful effect can be reduced by using solder containing a small quantity of copper, such as Multicore Savbit solder alloy.

To remove the possibility of copper erosion several manufacturers now supply iron-plated or nickel-coated tips for their irons. When new these must be tinned in the usual way immediately they are hot enough to melt the solder, otherwise they could possibly be spoilt by oxidisation. The iron coating is very tough and wears well. The tip should never be filed otherwise the iron coating will be lost and defeat the whole purpose of it being there in the first place. It is not necessary to use special solders containing copper with this type of bit.

During soldering the tip of the iron is covered with oxidised solder, resin flux and general dirt. To produce the best joints the iron must be kept perfectly clean and the working part of the tip shiny. This can be ensured by rubbing the iron tip on a piece of damp sponge (not plastic foam as it will just melt) or felt, prior to making a joint.

Several types of solder are available but for electronics work a tin/lead alloy (60/40) is used almost exclusively. The flux, which is necessary to keep the work clean during soldering and make the solder flow easily, is contained in cores throughout the length of solder. Thus the correct amount of flux is always applied to the joint with the solder. It dissolves oxides of metals but not grease. The work, therefore, has to be cleaned free of grease before use. Nickel platings (used on

6

some solder tags) should be removed with a smooth file to reveal the brass base, otherwise soldering may be difficult. Good solder flow over the entire surface area of the join is called *wetting*.

Two sizes of solder wire are in general use for this kind of work: 18 s.w.g. for large joints and 22 s.w.g. for circuit boards and other fine work. By using this fine solder (22 s.w.g.), there is less tendency to apply excess solder to a joint. In any case surplus solder should be removed by careful manipulation of the soldering iron.

When soldering to tags, the wire is looped on to the tag and squeezed with the pliers to give some mechanical strength. The solder is then placed on the tag and the iron applied on top of the solder (Fig. 1). The

Fig. 1. Soldering

When soldering a component to a tag, the hot iron should be pressed onto the workpiece. When it reaches the correct temperature, the solder flows and 'wets' the metal, forming the connection. Remove the iron and allow the joint to cool slowly. Solder joints on a p.c.b. are made in the same way, but for small copper areas the component lead and solder are heated together.

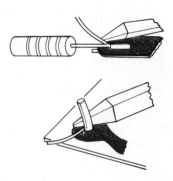

solder is heated with the tag and wire and melts; when the tag is at the correct temperature the solder will suddenly flow into the joint. At this stage more solder is fed in if the joint so requires. The iron should be removed as quickly as possible or the flux and solder may burn and excessive heat may be passed on through the connection to the component.

The joint must not be disturbed while cooling and the completed joint should be shiny and smooth. Any signs of 'graininess' of the surface indicates a poor joint, probably caused by movement or rapid cooling and it should be reheated.

Soldering to a printed circuit board is a little different in that the joint is sometimes too small to sandwich the solder between the iron and the joint. The iron can be 'wetted' with a small amount of solder and applied to the joint at the same time, taking care to heat both the component lead and the copper foil. The joint will heat very quickly and the solder can be fed to the junction of the component lead and the foil. The solder should flow quickly round the joint and the iron can then be removed.

Care must be taken not to overheat the joint otherwise burning can occur; the copper foil can melt away and damage can be caused to delicate components. Many commercial boards as supplied with kits have a coating of *solder resist* on them. This limits the flow of solder to the area surrounding the actual joint. These areas are also coated with a flux lacquer to protect and assist soldering, as well as to keep dirt and air out.

All component wires should preferably be cut to length before soldering, leaving about 3/32 in (2 mm) above the foil on the board, or about ¼ in (6 mm) bare for tag joints, as the strain of trimming wires afterwards could weaken the joint. Leads should be left perpendicular to the board if possible for easy removal later, but a slight bend can be made to hold the component captive (Fig. 2).

Fig. 2. Mounting components

Component leads may be left straight for easy subsequent removal from the board or slightly bent to hold the component captive while soldering

To prevent damage to delicate or heat-sensitive components (transistors, diodes, thermistors, etc.) a pair of small pliers can be used as a heat shunt. Commercial heat shunt clips are also available. The pliers should grip the wire between the joint and the component body.

Fig. 3. Forming component leads

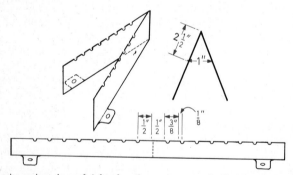

This handy gadget is useful for forming component leads prior to insertion in a printed circuit board. A piece of 16 s.w.g. (1.6 mm) aluminium or mild steel, approximately 1 in (25 mm) wide and 12 in (30 cm) long, with notches cut into one edge, is used. One clear inch should be left in the middle, ½ in (12 mm) either side of the bend. The strip is bent so that the separation is 1 in (25 mm) at 2½ in (64 mm) from the bend

8

This desoldering tip is designed to melt the solder for all pins of an integrated circuit package at the same time

When bending component leads it is important not to bend them too near the component otherwise a seal may be broken or the wire may break away. If possible, the component end of the lead should be held with a pair of round-nosed pliers while bending.

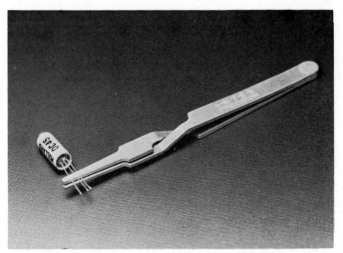

Heat shunt tweezers by Antex, intended to hold transistors and other sensitive components while soldering, to conduct some of the heat away from the device

When building kits or using matrix board, it will be found that the lead spacing is in multiples of 0.1 in (2.5 mm) or 0.15 in (3.8 mm). A simple gadget that can be made to ease the accurate bending of wires is shown in Fig. 3. Most small transistors have their lead-out wires so close together that they must be spread out to fit, otherwise the area of copper for each connection would be too small. To assist with this spreading and ensure a neat job, transistor mounting pads are used. Sockets are available for mounting transistors and integrated circuits,

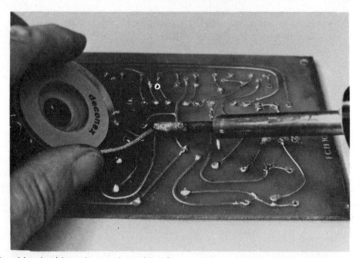

Desolder braid soaks up the solder from a joint when the joint and braid are heated together with a soldering iron, enabling the component to be easily removed from the p.c.b. (courtesy Decon Laboratories Ltd.)

which save the problems of soldering and desoldering and allow easy replacement. In any case the wires must not be bent closer than 2 mm from the point of entry into the body.

Small delicate devices, such as glass diodes or precision resistors, are best mounted with a loop in the leads as this lessens the risk of heat damage during soldering and protects the components from vibrations of the board.

Desoldering

There often arises the need for desoldering components—either by way of maintenance and service or to salvage useful parts. When desoldering, care has to be exercised not to overheat the joint or the solder will burn and not flow properly.

Another desoldering tool with a suction bulb. This model, the Adcola R500, has a special solder chamber that can be opened for cleaning out

To desolder components from tags is difficult if the wires are wrapped round them. Often three hands could be usefully employed to hold the iron, the workpiece and to unravel the wire. Cutting the component

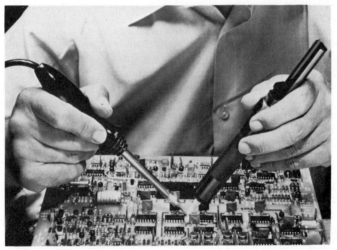

The piston type of desolder tool in use on a complex printed circuit board containing a number of dual-in-line integrated circuit packages. It sucks molten solder from the joint when the spring-loaded piston is released by pressing a button on the cylinder. Shown here in use with the Oryx thermostatic iron, both from Greenwood Electronics

free is often the best or only solution. However, if the leads are straight it is easy to warm up the tag and withdraw the wire. Solder can be removed from the component lead by heating it and wiping it clean. Solder can be removed from the tag by using 'desolder braid' which

A loop in the lead of delicate components reduces stress due to soldering and vibration

quickly draws all the solder away by capillary action. This useful aid is a copper braiding charged with a flux agent. Stripped screen braid from old but clean coaxial cable could be used.

Desolder braid is also most useful for desoldering printed circuit boards and is available in many widths to suit varying sizes of joint. The braid removes most of the solder from the joint, so allowing multi-pin devices to be removed in the minimum of time and with no damage to either the component or the board.

Several manufacturers produce specialised desolder tools which make a most useful addition to any tool kit. Operation is quick, the solder being sucked through a small orifice in the tip of the tool by releasing a small rubber bulb.

2 Kits and component buying

Electronics projects must sometimes seem to have an uncertain future for many beginners. However, a feeling of confidence is soon built up which enables one to tackle almost any project—no matter how large. To build up this confidence, the early projects must be completed with a degree of success and without too many setbacks. To ensure a fair chance of success the beginner could consider building reasonably simple published designs or kits. Very soon, confidence will be gained along with a desire to have a go at the more complex projects published in the popular electronics magazines.

The term *kit* is often used by suppliers or manufacturers as a box full of the required parts to build a specific project, usually with a copy of the circuit details where available. If the company has gone to great trouble to produce a kit of this sort, one ought to expect the basic design to be sound. If a ready-drilled printed circuit board is included, made specially to the original design, then there should be few, if any, problems. Some firms include cabinets in their kits, but leave the actual assembly and finishing to the constructor.

Kits are available in which all the metalwork has been completed, the panels finished and even lettered to a professional appearance. The end result gives the impression that it is made from parts taken from a production line, together with a comprehensive assembly manual.

This type of kit is useful where the completed item is to have a specific task and must perform reliably for a number of years (for example, audio equipment and test gear). Usually a specification is published to which completed kits should perform when made up according to the instructions; often its performance turns out better than the specification. A good after-sales service is essential so that advice can be obtained if necessary. Critical sub-assemblies are often supplied ready assembled and aligned.

The range of kits available is vast and the choice can be somewhere between a modest bag of components for part or the whole project, up to a comprehensive service to help you get your chosen project completed successfully. The constructor should investigate all of the implications in the kit service offered, including the possibility of technical help from the right authority.

The fact that kit suppliers' catalogues include a wide range of projects must show that constructors of all abilities can find a project to suit

Simple transistor tester built from a basic kit prepared by Doram Electronics. All components are supplied but the constructor is free to prepare his own style of front panel

them, this often being the only way to obtain a specific item at an economic cost. Items of test equipment available range from simple multimeters to wideband oscilloscopes, alignment generators and function generators. Of course, the truly amateur constructor will want to do the job entirely on his own, but if there is not a suitable design to hand, or maybe special cabinet making is called for, then a kit offers a useful alternative. The components and other parts supplied in kits are often of a high standard and, where an instruction manual is provided, the details are usually explicit. A detailed description of circuit operation and fault-finding hints are very useful for subsequent reference if failure or breakdown ever occurs.

Audio amplifier kit assembled from a Josty Kit MT20. The constructor is left to provide his own cabinet

All the parts of a Heathkit solid state multimeter, including the metalwork, a case, test leads and two detailed instruction manuals

15

High quality test equipment can be built at home without special tools. This is the Heathkit double beam oscilloscope assembled and ready to use

Somewhere between kits and assembled equipment is the modular form of construction, sometimes referred to as kits but of a different sort. These enable the constructor to build a system incorporating the required features of ready-made modules that he can connect together

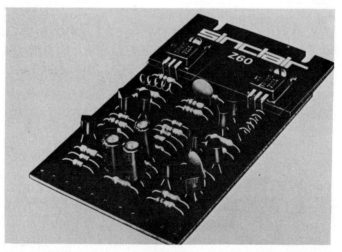

Kits can comprise a number of ready made modules that the constructor links together. An example is the Sinclair Project scheme. This is the Z60 amplifier module which is used in Project 80

as he requires at fairly low cost. These modules are linked by following the instructions that should be provided.

Before any electronics project can be started, apart from kits, components must be obtained. As time goes by, the constructor will find himself accumulating a stock of various commonly used components although these will rarely complete his needs for a specific project without further purchase. The various magazines available carry a large number of advertisements for component suppliers large and small. Generally they follow a fairly consistent pricing structure so that little difference is seen between suppliers for the most common items.

When ordering components by post, it helps to reduce paperwork and postage by ordering as much as possible from one supplier. How much actually arrives, and the waiting time involved, varies enormously

For less experienced constructors, the Sinclair Project 805, which can be assembled without soldering by using simple push-tags

but constructors will find from experience who best serves their needs. Most of the best suppliers are very quick and maintain reasonable stock levels. However, it is very important and helpful to send a clear and concise order, without other queries, on one large sheet of typing paper, including your full name address, telephone number and remittance details; in some cases a credit card number can be quoted where acceptable to avoid uncertainties about payment.

It must be remembered that, on receipt of an order, the components have to be located from different parts of a stock room; obviously it is easier if an accurate description of the components is given. Where

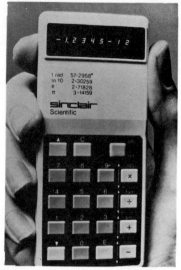

This kit for this calculator can be assembled in a couple of hours on the double-sided, 'through-hole' plated board supplied

catalogues are used, quote the stock number and description; the page number should be shown separately to avoid mistakes.

It is equally important to make sure that the financial side of the order is correct. The total should be clearly shown, the postage or carriage charge added plus V.A.T. at the current rate, unless V.A.T. inclusive prices are given. The V.A.T. must be sufficient to cover that

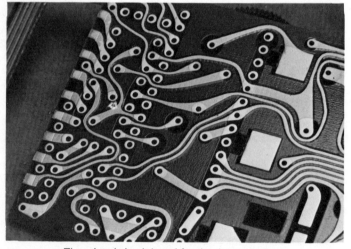

The printed circuit board for the above calculator

on carriage and packing charges as well as on the total goods value.

Experience will soon show which suppliers keep a good stock and are able to offer a quick and reliable service. Isolated cases of poor service do occur, but are not always necessarily indicative of a poor supplier. There are numerous reasons why orders cannot be met as promptly as one might expect. Personal visits when possible are always preferable for satisfactory results.

An interesting point to note is that the price of some components offered to the amateur constructor are in many cases below the apparent

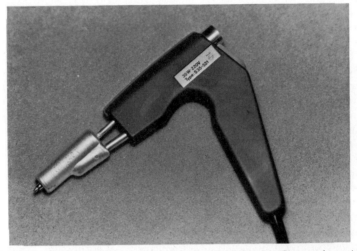

Specially designed desolder tools, such as those described in Chapter 1, or this Philips instrument that allows quick hand operation, enable components to be salvaged easily from 'ex-computer' and similar printed circuit assemblies

industrial price structure. These may be quite genuine offers of components to specified standards or they may be special offers of serviceable but outside manufacturer's specification samples. You should satisfy yourself of the standard of goods that you order as it is often difficult or costly to rectify any possible error or misunderstanding on your part.

To locate special items can require scrutiny of the advertisements. If the item you require cannot be found, more diligent enquiries may be necessary. Often a published design may specify a seemingly obscure item; usually if the supplier is not quoted then the publisher or magazine staff can help. Special project-linked advertisements are published after the project has appeared.

It is possible to purchase batches of mixed surplus components at

19

low prices; these can often turn out to be of good value, but the purchaser must be prepared for mixed quality goods. The best of a batch can be selected by simple tests with a multimeter (further details in Chapter 8).

Capacitors are often available and, if all the correct markings are present on the case, one can reasonably expect them to be usable. Electrolytic types do not store well and sometimes have to be disposed of through various channels when they risk deterioration. The problem is usually high leakage current and a selection of these should be checked before use (see Chapter 8). A high leakage factor usually improves with use.

Many unmarked but tested transistors are available at attractive prices and are often described as similar to a particular known type. This similarity is seldom specific enough to tell of its likely performance. However, the transistors may be usable in experimental circuits, but a simple transistor tester should be used to see if the samples have a useful current gain, say, greater than 30 or 40 (see Chapter 8). The maximum voltage of these transistors is rather vague, but they are usually satisfactory with supplies up to about 15 V or so, even if the normal equivalent is specified as higher. For critical applications, properly marked transistors should save damage and frustration in an otherwise satisfactory circuit. The markings should include the manufacturer's trade mark and type number.

Ex-equipment printed circuit boards are often offered at low prices and if one has a good desolder tool and plenty of patience, the transistors and other components can be salvaged for use in projects with some cost saving. Sometimes the transistor types are obscure, so a data book should be consulted before using them.

The home constructor may not want to get involved with the metalwork to produce a case. It is easier to buy an off-the-shelf item from one of the many suppliers of ready-made cases. The cost is reasonable and the finish often better than can be achieved with limited resources. Usually the front panels are finished in a neutral colour so that any type of finish can be applied over the top, with lettering to suit. However, where custom design cases are necessary to the designs followed the reader will find further details in *Project Planning and Building*.

The local ironmonger or d.i.y. shop can supply hardware fittings, nuts and bolts, etc. Some mail order firms specialise in supplying the nuts and bolts, cables, grommets and labels or even undertake the fabrication of a panel to the constructor's requirements.

Occasionally constructional projects specify particular components which may be difficult to find. Unless a special note is given on the supplier, one may be able to try a more readily available substitute.

Transistors can cause some confusion in this respect where one type may be used in place of another, but not *vice versa*. Reference to substitution tables should provide useful suggested replacement type numbers. Audio output and driver transistors, however, need to be chosen with care for high quality circuits—random substitution may give results far short of the target specification. High frequency types can be particularly difficult.

Capacitors are often not critical components, except where used in tuned circuits and phase-shift networks, where their values are of critical importance. This applies also to high frequency applications where ceramic types with low self-inductance are necessary. In other applications slightly higher capacitance values or higher voltage values are permissible.

Switches and controls may be substituted by near alternatives to those specified. See if it is possible to omit some facility if a different switch is to be used. Designers may specify 'ganged' controls on a common shaft. An example is the volume control and on-off switch. There is no reason why one should not use separate controls in this case; it could save wear and tear on the control. Two-way rotary switches can easily be replaced by push-buttons or toggle switches, and *vice versa*.

When introducing the personal touch by modifying a suggested design, it improves the sense of self-satisfaction on completion, which in turn builds confidence. The constructor should modify a design with great care, particularly in critical performance circuits, lest the performance is likely to be changed. The designer is not likely to be able to advise in this event if the project fails.

3 Layout and wiring

An electronic circuit diagram is a simplified representation of how the components of a circuit are connected together. The diagram may be a clumsy way of laying out the components but nevertheless would produce a working model, assuming that stray capacitance did not upset its intended operation. Detailed guidance on circuit diagrams can be found in the Constructor's Guide on *Electronic Diagrams*.

When a circuit is built up on tags the connection points can be reduced to less than the number shown on the drawing, while with a printed circuit board layout the number of connection points may well be more.

Conventionally, drawings show the positive and negative power rails running along the top and bottom of the page. This makes for easier 'sight reading' of the circuit diagram, but if we can break these rules a more compact circuit layout can be achieved. An example of this is the p.c.b. for a commercial transistor radio; this usually looks nothing like the circuit diagram and power rails—the longest continuous conductors —can be seen to weave around the board.

It is important to remember that stray capacitance exists between adjacent pairs of conductors. This can cause unwanted coupling of signals and so in critical (for example radio) applications conductors must be kept well separated. An earthed screen between the conductors electrically removes the coupling and this is the main reason for using screened leads for sensitive audio and r.f. wiring.

The capacitance between two 1 in (25 mm) lengths of solid connecting wire twisted together is about 6 pF to 8 pF, and between two parallel 0.1 in (2.5 mm) p.c.b. tracks 5 in long, spaced by 0.05 in, is about 4 pF to 5 pF.

There are three general types of layout, 'point-to-point' 'nuclear' and 'meshed' layout. The latter two are mostly used for p.c.b.s.

Point-to-point wiring follows the circuit diagram fairly closely. This type of wiring is usually applied to tag strips (Fig. 4). Reducing

Fig. 4. Wiring Layout

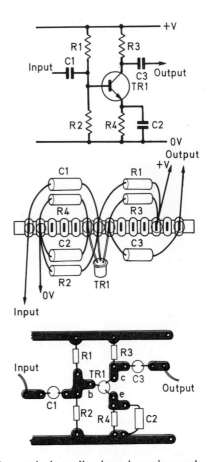

This simple common emitter amplifier stage can be built on a tag strip to have only seven connections while on a printed circuit board nineteen soldered joints have to be made

the number of connections to be made is easily done by using each tag as the only connector for all components to that point. Obviously two tags may be joined to accommodate more components.

Point-to-point is a useful way of laying out prototype circuits, especially on perforated board with wire or copper strip interconnections. The layout is relatively simple to design and easy to follow when trouble-shooting.

As the earth lead for a circuit is usually continuous it is convenient to make this the 'nucleus' of the board, with all components leading out towards the power rail which forms the perimeter of the board. Conversely, a popular way is to form the earth strip around the perimeter and the components leading towards the central area. *Nuclear layout* is very compact and eliminates most 'earthing' difficulties of which more will be said later.

Mesh layout is the most common commercial p.c.b. layout technique. In this way earth and power rails entwine so that they are available anywhere on the board. By this method the greatest component packing

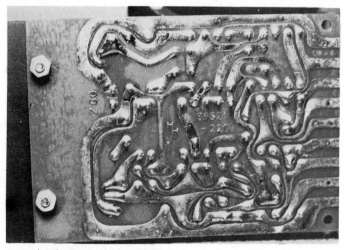

An example of commercial 'mesh' type of p.c.b. layout; edge connection points are shown on the right. This the underside of the Sinclair Z60 amplifier

density is achieved, making a very compact layout possible. The completed layout usually bears no resemblence to the original circuit diagram at all, which makes servicing difficult unless a layout is available. Designing a layout of this kind is very difficult.

With all layouts care has to be taken to minimise difficulties caused by earth and power returns. Any conductor has a resistance and consequently, when passing current, drops a very small voltage along its length. In a good layout the voltage drop is so small that it does not interfere with the designed operation of the circuit. However, in a careless layout, it is possible for the voltage drop on output or power supply lines to appear at the input of an amplifier, giving rise to some fear of instability or distortion. Illustrated examples of earth return problems are shown with possible solutions in Fig. 5.

24

Fig. 5. Earth returns

Fig. 5a. The output current from the power amplifier flows through the loudspeaker and through the wiring A to B to the negative supply terminal. The length of conductor A to C is also part of the input circuit and the voltage dropped along A—C due to the output current will be fed to the preamp. input together with the tuner signal. The result may be distortion or instability

Fig. 5b. In this layout the power supply current for the power amplifier flows along D to E and any changes in current, brought about by the amplifier producing an output, result in a signal being fed to the power amplifier input, giving rise to distortion or instability

Fig. 5c. A correctly assembled system utilises a main earth tie point to which all earth returns are taken. In this way voltage drops along connecting leads are isolated from signal lines resulting in a stable system. Power supply decoupling from the preamplifier is affected by resistor R and capacitor C. By returning C to the earth tie point, ripple and supply rail components should not upset system operation.

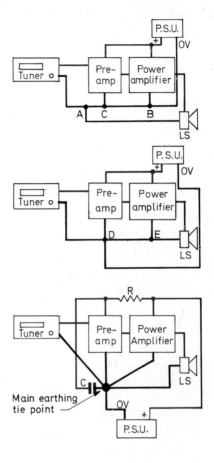

Digital or switching currents take very rapid pulses of current from the supply and if these are reflected on the earth line due to bad layout, the logic may function in an erratic manner. Fortunately, most logic families have a safe working margin called the *noise immunity* within which p.c.b. layout requirements are easily accommodated.

Power supply lines are often *decoupled* to reduce a.c. voltage fluctuations which could upset circuit operation. A capacitor (the decoupling capacitor) provides a short-circuit path for a.c. to the earth line; quite a high current can flow in this capacitor. It is therefore important to earth the capacitor at the main earth terminal point, otherwise ripple could be introduced into the signal lines, perhaps with worse results than if no decoupling had been used.

With high frequency circuits the tiny inductance of connecting leads becomes more important than their resistance. V.H.F. radio circuits always need to be laid out with great care to avoid earthing troubles and also capacitive coupling, which is very much more troublesome than at audio frequencies. R.F. circuits always have a central earth point to which all decoupling capacitors and earth leads are connected and are contained in an earthed metal screened enclosure to prevent radiation or pick-up. Instability is a common fault with v.h.f. circuits and can arise in an otherwise satisfactory design for the following reasons:

Stray capacitance—Unwanted coupling between components, wiring or circuit sections; earthed metal screening can effectively reduce capacitive coupling.

Stray inductive coupling—Unwanted coupling between sections; a few turns of wire near a second wire produces an efficient transformer coupling at very high frequencies.

Earthing arrangements:

Power supply not properly decoupled—Some capacitors produce inductive effects and may hinder rather than assist. Use disc ceramic types where possible.

Metal can of transistor not earthed—V.H.F. transistors usually provide a lead (screen) to earth the can.

Two feed-through capacitors used to supply from one screened circuit to another while acting as decoupling capacitors in a u.h.f. tuner

Feed-through capacitors are often used for decoupling in r.f. circuits and typically have a capacitance of 1nF (1000pF) and only a tiny inductance. The outer case is push-fitted or soldered to the screen metal-work (if earthed) or the earthed copper of the p.c.b. Usually they are used for a.c. decoupling of supply lines and carrying this supply to the other side of the metal or p.c.b. but are also useful for any decoupling operation. Their quoted capacitance value is only nominal and can deviate considerably, so they should not be used in tuned circuits or for timing purposes.

A large portion of construction time for any project is spent wiring controls in as neat a way as possible. Solid single strand wire is usually used for neatness although it should not be used where any movement will be anticipated, otherwise the conductor will break; thin stranded wire should be used instead.

The wires from each control can be twisted together or they may all be run together and routed in a *cable harness*. The wires should be colour coded for identification or labels may be used. The harness may

Bundles of wire can be neatly 'tied' into a harness by using this plastics coil known as 'spiral-wrap' or Spirap

be held together with traditional looping with waxed twine but modern spiral wrapping is effective and easier to fit and allows for subsequent alterations without upsetting the form.

When stranded wires from controls are to be soldered to a p.c.b., it is necessary that the strands be twisted together and tinned with solder before being inserted into the board otherwise 'whiskers' of wire may not go through the hole and may short to nearby components or copper pads.

27

The greatest problem with wiring up switches lies in identifying the various connections. An ohmmeter is an invaluable aid to establish the

Cable markers are useful for identification of wires in a cable form; they can be obtained in a variety of sizes and codes

switching mode and all connections should be verified before construction to avoid mistakes.

A switch is described in terms of poles and ways. The number of ways is the number of positions that the switch wiper contact can rest in. Examples are illustrated in Fig. 6.

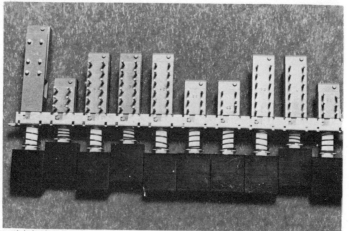

A multiple bank of push-button switches designed for mounting on a printed circuit board

Fig. 6. Switches

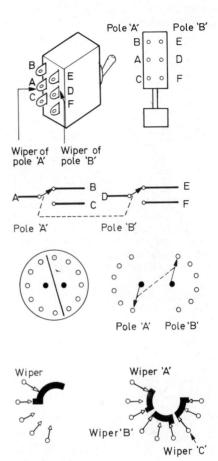

Fig. 6a. Toggle and slide switch connections often closely represent the connections on the circuit diagram, as shown in this example of a 2-pole 2-way switch

Fig. 6b. This simple 2-pole 6-way switch has its contacts laid out in a logical, easy-to-follow manner. The position of the end stops is easily located with an ohmmeter

Fig. 6c. Part of the wafer switch contact assembly, showing 1-pole 4-way on the left and 3-pole 2-way on the right. The wiper is easily located as it is the longest contact permanently brushing the central ring

Slide and toggle switches are usually self-explanatory but sometimes a switch may have more poles than is required. It is fairly simple to sort out which switch contacts are not needed.

The contact slide in some toggle switches moves down when the toggle moves down—others move up. This can only be verified with a meter. Should the wiring turn out to be inverted, it is a simple matter to turn the switch through 180°. American, Japanese and some other countries in Europe use the conventional down position for 'off'; the converse to British practice. Some imported switches with label plates

29

may reflect this, so do not think an error has been made until you can check the correct functions with a meter.

There are two types of rotary switch—the easy and the difficult. The 'easy' switches are supplied as a complete assembly ready to wire up, while the more difficult are the wafer assembly kits that can be made up by the constructor to suit his needs.

The simple rotary switch is usually built upon a 12-position mechanism. The combinations available are 1-pole 12-way, 2-pole 6-way,

A rotary wafer switch assembly comprising two banks, each of 4-pole 3-ways, two poles on each side

3-pole 4-way, 4-pole 3-way, 6-pole 2-way. When asking for a 1-pole 4-way, a 1-pole 12-way is usually supplied. Sometimes adjustable stops are provided to limit the rotation to four positions; the other eight

One of the above wafers shown separately. Note the central rotary wiper ring and the wiper contacts at top-left and lower-right

being superfluous could be used to mount other small components, provided that no switch connection is made.

The switch wipers are usually the tags in the centre of the switch with the contacts positioned round the perimeter. The switch can resemble the representation on a circuit diagram. The tag corresponding to the end stop of rotation is found with an ohmmeter—the others simply follow round in sequence.

Wafer assemblies require a little detective work to find their connections. A single wafer can have one or more switches on the front and on the reverse side as well. In a case such as this the tags around the perimeter alternately belong to the front and back of the wafer. Several wafers can be built up on a single shaft to produce really complex units, each being simultaneously operated by the common rotary shaft.

The common shaft assembly gives twelve positions per full rotation but others available give 6, 10, 15, 18, 22, 25 or even 30. Obviously the correct corresponding wafers must be used with them.

The switch functions by rotating the inner portion of the wafer to make contact through the wiper ring and the shorter contact tags as it turns. Contact is made to the wiper by the longest contact tag which remains in contact with the central ring for all positions of the shaft. This is clearly shown in Fig. 6c.

Several such assemblies can be built up on each side of a wafer to give multiple poles. The long contact tags are the wiper connections and by inspection when operating the shaft you can see which are the corresponding switch contacts. Great care has to be taken when wiring these switches as mistakes are easily made.

To save p.c.b. space components are often mounted directly onto the switch wafers, using the contact tags as if they were part of tag strip. Dummy wafers (without centre rings) can also be used to assist in mounting components.

Screened leads prevent the inner conductor being subjected to capacitive pick-up provided that the screen is earthed. For audio applications the screen is used solely for this purpose.

Screened leads become more necessary as the impedance of the appropriate part of the circuit rises. Generally, most audio wiring over 3 in (75 mm) long, especially near the mains supply leads, power supply or speaker wiring, should be screened. The screen should be connected at one end only; usually the easiest to arrange is at the socket end, to avoid creating hum problems due to an earth loop. This occurs when multiple connections are made to 'earthing' points causing instability or buzz in mains operated equipment.

Fig. 7 shows how a number of audio inputs are wired into an amplifier considered liable to give earth return troubles. It can be seen that at the input sockets all braidings are connected together and to the main earth tie point. The screened leads carrying the signals to the preamplifier have their braidings earthed *only* at the input end. To earth a braiding at the preamplifier end as well would create an earth loop with its attendant difficulties.

Fig. 7. Screened leads

To avoid earth loop problems, the input sockets for an audio amplifier each have their screens connected to 'earth' at the main earth tie point only. The screen of each signal lead is connected to earth at one end only and in this case it is most convenient to earth the braids to the input sockets

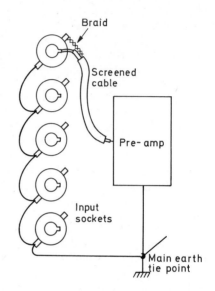

Braid

Screened cable

Pre-amp

Input sockets

Main earth tie point

Screened cable typically has a capacitance of 100 pF per foot length measured between the centre core and the screen. This is effectively in parallel with the signal path and can reduce the level of high frequencies when fed from a high impedance source. One effective method to prevent severe problems of this sort upsetting the performance of the equipment is to use emitter-follower stages to feed the signals over low impedance lines to the controls; screened cable is not necessary in these circumstances.

Most audio plugs allow for the metal casing to be connected to the braiding, so screening the pin connections. DIN standard plugs conventionally have pin 2 (centre pin) connected to the braiding but to reduce buzz the metal shroud can also be connected to the braiding. This is easily done by dividing the braid strands into two bundles—one for connection to pin 2 and the other to the screen.

Loudspeakers are not generally wired with screened cable as they are of low impedance and are not prone to stray pick-up; screened cable for this application could cause an appreciable voltage drop.

The braiding of r.f. coaxial cable prevents the signal being radiated and lost (i.e. the line behaving as a transmitting aerial) and also gives the line a characteristic impedance. For example, television cable is nominally 75 ohms in the U.K. (300 ohms in some other countries). To recover the signal from the line at the receiver end with minimal loss, the load impedance must be the same. The signal must be fed into the line from a 75 ohm (or 300 ohm) aerial array as appropriate. Coaxial cable is termed as being unbalanced as the signal is transmitted at a voltage with respect to earth (the braiding). It is possible to transmit a signal down a balanced line in which earth plays no part or is made the neutral point of reference matched exactly with respect to both lines; these being in opposite phase. The advantage of this is that any noise picked up on one conductor is balanced by an opposing voltage on the other and so cancels out. The line is non-transmitting and so does not usually need to be screened.

Most aerial systems in the U.K. are 75 ohms (for television and radio) but facilities can be provided to enable 300 ohm feeder to be used. Similarly 300 ohm balanced inputs on receivers can be used with 75 ohm aerial if the correct matching device is used. This can take the form of a small v.h.f. transformer or *balun*, which is a simple means of using coaxial cable of precisely measured characteristics. More detailed information on this subject can be found in a good aerial handbook (for instance *The Practical Aerial Handbook*, by Gordon J. King, published by Newnes-Butterworths).

4 Wiring boards

With the use of modern miniature components almost all wiring is reduced to easy-to-use wiring boards or printed circuit boards. To remove the need to design and make p.c.b.s for individual projects, several manufacturers offer a form of *matrix board* with a standard arrangement of holes and often a 'universal' layout of copper conductors on the wiring side. A typical example is *Veroboard,* now well established in a range of styles and sizes for both amateur and professional use.

Standard Veroboard has holes spaced by either 0.1 in (2.5 mm) or 0.15 in (3.8 mm) pitch. The 0.1 in size is useful for integrated circuits which have similar pin spacing, and for compact layouts. Beginners are recommended to try the 0.15 in pitch board first as the possibility of making mistakes or spoiling a layout is reduced.

Designs that are published to make use of Veroboard usually show a view of the component layout and either a list of hole positions for connections and/or cuts in the copper strips, or a view of the copper side showing the parallel copper conductors with connections and cuts marked. The conductors on a new board run the full length of the board without a break. In some designs the conductors are broken into several insulated sections by using a hand tool known as a *spot-face cutter* or by carefully cutting with a sharp knife. The spot-face cutter has a tip with cutting blades like those on a twist drill and a locating spigot in the centre. The spigot is inserted in a hole and the tool is rotated by hand on the copper surrounding the hole until the conductor is completely severed. It is a good idea to cut all the necessary conductors before actually mounting components as the breaks serve as landmarks or reference points. If cutting is attempted later, solder may prevent a clean cut being made.

34

Each hole or location on a board is referred to by its co-ordinate position code. Rows are usually lettered from A to Z and the columns are numbered. Each component can therefore be given a reference position for each connection, for example, 13R, 5E and so on.

Small components (resistors, capacitors, diodes) can be fitted so that their wires are bent or formed to pass through the correct holes. After soldering, the surplus wire is snipped off. It is very important to check that no solder bridges adjacent copper pads or wires. The boards

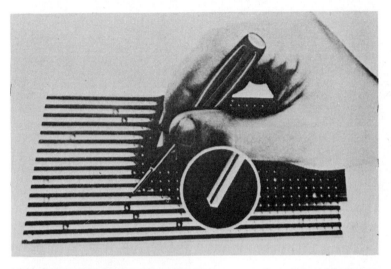

A spot-face cutter is used to remove the copper surrounding a hole on Veroboard, thus breaking the continuity of the copper strip

are coated with a thin flux which makes soldering very easy, but by touching the iron briefly onto another track one can easily create a solder 'bridge'. The easiest way to proceed is to remove all solder from the joint (desolder braid is perhaps the easiest way) and remake the joint. It is surprising how quickly projects can be thus assembled. With care and discreet application of solder, the finished result can be of neat appearance.

It is relatively easy to convert a circuit diagram into a Veroboard layout, especially if one adopts a similar layout. Some guidance on this aspect can be found in the Constructor's Guide on *Simple Circuit Building.* It is best to have the copper tracks of the Veroboard running horizontally with the power and earth rails near the top and bottom of the board; a couple of tracks left between these lines and the board edges are useful for mounting or for acting as extra long links from one end of the board to the other where they need to be kept away from other connections. It is then fairly straightforward to place the components in a similar relative position to that which they occupy on the circuit diagram.

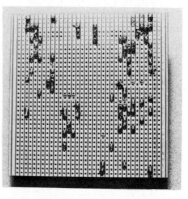

Underside view of a typical Veroboard layout on 0.1in matrix copper clad board. Some breaks in the strips are shown in the middle. This example is of a Mullard design amplifier

Interconnections are taken care of by the copper tracks running underneath and on the reverse side of the board to the components. Sometimes wire links are needed to connect two strips together,

The component side of the above assembly. Note the wire link used in the centre, to link two strips

although this is only necessary when making a determined effort towards miniaturisation. Boards always look much neater with components laid along the rows of holes rather than at odd angles.

A less expensive method is to use perforated board without copper strips and make your own connections using thin tinned copper wire (20 or 22 s.w.g.) on the underside. Again the components can be

36

A stereo power amplifier built on plain perforated matrix board. Notice the matched layout on each half and the simple heatsink plates on the power output transistors

positioned on the board roughly following the layout of the circuit diagram; the supply rails are wired between pins at either end of the board. The rest of the components are then wired in, using their own connecting leads for support through the holes. Components with stiff leads are trimmed to provide stubs around which other wires may

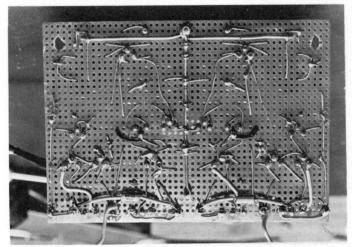

The underside view of the above assembly. Note the thick earth wire running down the centre, which acts as a single earth return point as is practicable

37

be wrapped and soldered. Crossover connections can be made if sleeving is fitted on one of the wires to avoid short-circuits.

Perforated matrix board is perhaps not the neatest possible form of wiring medium but is a quick means of assembling a circuit and is as reliable as the constructor's workmanship.

Component assembly board of 0.1 in pitch is suitable for dual-in-line (DIL) packages; i.c. holders are recommended for easy removal of the

A complex assembly of dual-in-line integrated circuits with extra components added. Notice the neat positioning of the interconnections, the key slot for an edge connector on the left and the power rail 'fingers' between the i.c.s

i.c. However, for complex layouts, special DIL boards are available which are designed to contain a number of packages mounted in neat rows. Plug-in edge connectors can be used with these.

Double-sided Veroboard for i.c.s has a standard 0.1 in matrix but conductor strips are provided on both sides of the board. These are arranged at right angles to each other, enabling complex layouts to be made with the integrated circuits packed closely together. Connections from one side of the board to the other are made by soldering the connections to both sides of the board. A short piece of wire on a *Veropin can be used for connection through the board and soldered on both sides.

The DIP breadboards have provision for mounting up to sixteen 8-, 14- or 16-pin DIL packages on a board. Connections between i.c.s are made using thin insulated connecting wire neatly arranged in the 'avenues' between the packages. Wiring is simply a matter of

38

following the circuit diagram or connection schedule and linking the appropriate copper pads for the i.c. pin numbers indicated.

The boards have power rails arranged as 'fingers' passing each package, often being conveniently positioned between the two rows of i.c. pin connections. Power is applied by wiring to the correct pin of each device. Disc ceramic decoupling capacitors (0.1 μF) can be connected between the fingers—possibly using eight for a full board layout.

Most types of *Veroboard can be plugged into an edge connector socket so that they can be removed for service. The standard connector pitch for this is 0.1 in (2.5 mm) or 0.15 in (3.8 mm); in the USA 0.156 in (3.96 mm) pitch is used.

Another form of strip board is the *Verostrip which is a long narrow board with rows of short copper pads along each long edge. These can be used as simple mounting strips for components in place of tag strips or to carry connecting wires. It is also suitable for applications where a group component board might be used, or for experimental integrated circuit work.

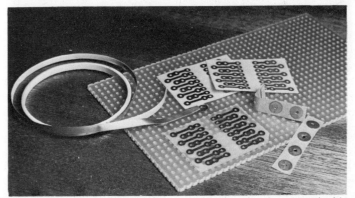

Copper symbol clusters are stuck down onto the board and connected with self-adhesive copper strips to build up a working layout of interconnections. These are 'Circuit-stik' samples

Invariably, wires from controls have to be connected to the board somewhere. The neatest way to do this is by soldering the wire to a pin inserted at the appropriate point. Otherwise the wire can be inserted directly through a hole and soldered just like the component wires. Stranded wire must be twisted and tinned before trying to insert it into the hole, otherwise odd strands might escape and short to nearby components. The layout is much neater if the connections are all brought to the edge of the board enabling the wires to be tied together in a harness form.

39

Using plain matrix board, a circuit can be built up by applying self-adhesive copper pads so that the holes in them coincide with the board holes. The pads are linked with similar strips of adhesive copper foil joined to them. The copper strips are made in roll form with a protective back film.

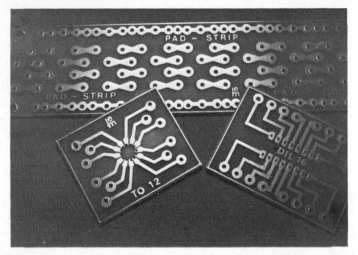

Prototype and experimental boards are handy for quick assembly and for trying out different circuit ideas. These are produced by H. M. Electronics and include easy connection pads for intricate i.c.s

A large selection of device 'clusters' (all connections for a single device) and additional shapes such as edge connectors and multiple DIL layouts are available. This system, commercially called *Circuit-stik, can be laid down on to a plain plastics sheet, such as s.r.b.p., glass-fibre or *Formica. The board is then drilled as required to accept component leads as dictated by the holes in the pads. Drilling can be arranged to one side of the pads if need be to avoid disturbing them.

The adhesive backing for these pads is very strong, but allows parts of the circuit to be repositioned if mistakes are made. Clusters and symbols cannot be repositioned with success if removed from the board after 24 hours as the adhesive is then fully cured.

Soldering is carried out in the normal way but, to be fair to the adhesive, careful application of the soldering iron should be exercised with the minimum necessary heat transfer. To assist the connection between a conductor strip and pad a solder bridge should be applied.

*Trade names.

40

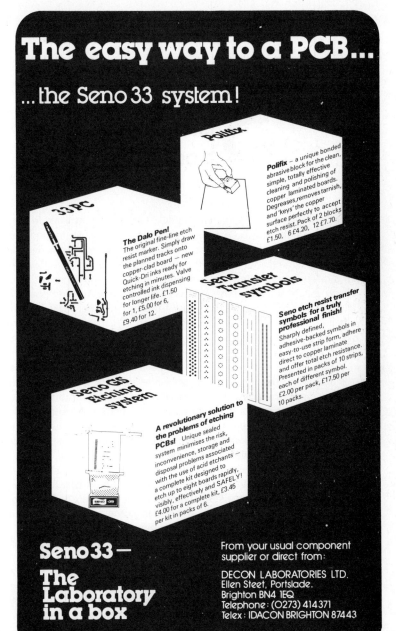

5 Printed circuit boards

Commercially most electronic equipment is assembled, at least in part, on printed circuit boards. A typical board has to be custom made for each job, which means that major modifications cannot be carried out without redesigning the board and rebuilding the assembly. However, minor alterations can often be carried out on an existing layout.

There are two main base materials generally available: phenolic resin paper (s.r.b.p.) and epoxy glass fibre board. The latter has the advantage of higher leakage resistance and is capable of operating in extreme environmental conditions, but is more expensive than the phenolic base. For most amateur or experimental applications, other than critical high voltage and high impedance circuits, s.r.b.p. base boards are quite adequate and, in fact easier to work with hand tools.

Printed circuit boards are laid out with component mounting holes positioned according to a 0.1 in (2.5 mm) grid matrix, although unlike Veroboard, not all hole positions on this are drilled out or used. Multi-lead components (e.g. skeleton presets, i.c. packages, transistors) have their leads formed to fit directly on to the grid.

Small resistors and capacitors (where possible) have 0.5 in (12.5 mm) spacing between mounting hole centres when horizontally mounted; this makes a neat and consistent layout. However, there is no reason why closer spacing should not be adopted commensurate with considerations of capacitive and inductive coupling.

For high density packing and miniaturisation, components often need to be mounted vertically on the board. Small resistors can have their leads spaced by as little as 0.1 in. Bulky components, such as large electrolytic capacitors, should be mounted horizontally if possible, otherwise a sharp shock to the board could possibly dislodge the component wires. There is no rigid ruling on this point and, indeed, many of these components of, say 220 μF, can be mounted vertically.

Copper is, of course, a good conductor of heat and use can be made of an area of copper as a heat sink for a component. An area of 10 cm^2 can serve as a heatsink for stud mounted diodes or thyristors. This method of cooling is popular for some of the medium power audio integrated circuit packages, which have especially wide legs to assist heat transfer to the copper foil.

A more detailed account of different characteristics and applications of printed circuit boards can be found in the Constructor's Guide on *Printed Circuit Assembly,* a companion volume in this series. Here we shall look at processing methods that constructors can try out for themselves.

There are several ways of making a printed circuit pattern but before processing can be carried out the board must be cut to size and thoroughly cleaned. The copper surface soon becomes tarnished and oxidised when exposed to the air. A badly tarnished board can be cleaned with scouring powder and finally polished with fine wire

Glass fibre brushes are the most effective way of removing copper tarnish and polishing the surface prior to processing of the p.c.b. (courtesy Eraser International Ltd)

wool or a hard fibre brush. A clean, carefully stored board should just need polishing; any residue of cleaning agent must be completely removed.

The p.c.b. process involves covering the copper that is to remain on the board with etchant resist and etching the exposed copper away in a chemical bath. The etchant resist is then removed leaving the copper areas exposed ready to be drilled for the components.

The design for the conductors can be laid out on the copper using a fine paint brush and enamel paint. Using carbon paper, trace the design from the original layout pattern on to the copper surface. The carbon outline is then painted over very carefully with the paint which is allowed to dry before etching (Fig. 8). It is helpful to leave very small

Fig. 8. Paint as resist

When using paint as a resist there is little point in the delicate brushwork necessary to leave a minimum of copper on the board. Large copper 'lands' result in lower resistance and more reliable adhesion with less risk of fracture

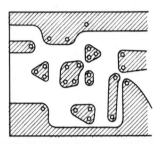

circles in the drilling positions to identify and ease the drilling later. Alternatively, press a compass point into the copper through the layout drawing at each component hole location before painting. This ensures that each hole will be surrounded by sufficient copper to make a sound joint as well as making sure that the holes will be accurately drilled.

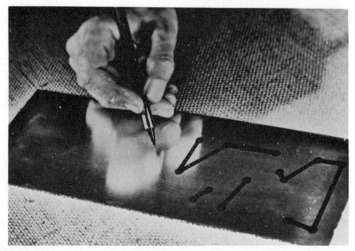

A resist pen enables a conductor design to be quickly laid out on to a clean copper board (courtesy Decon Laboratories Ltd.)

After etching (described later) the paint is easily removed with paint stripper and the board washed and well dried to prevent oxidisation before use.

There are a number of pens available that apply an even coating of resist paint on to the copper surface. The paint in the 'Pentel' type markers is cellulose based and is very quick drying. After etching it can be removed by applying paint stripper.

Several companies distribute pens specially designed for p.c.b. preparation, which have a fine tip to allow intricate designs to be laid out without much difficulty. The line width is normally about 1.5 mm. The resist is removed from the board after etching (or to correct mistakes) using a solvent such as trichloroethylene. This gives off a harmful vapour and must be used in a well ventilated room. One advantage of these layout pens is that a ruler can be used with them for straight line pads (Fig. 9). A convenient way to work is to to prick the

Fig. 9. Using resist pens

Resist pens produce a very neat layout when used with a ruler to give straight lines. The first stage is to mark the position of component mounting holes by sticking a compass point into the copper at each pad location. The pad is then drawn in, bearing in mind that pad size will be slightly smaller due to under-etching, and the pads connected by straight lines

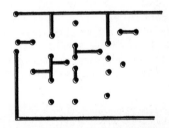

copper at each interconnection point and surround this with resist from the pen. These areas will form the solder pads on the finished board.

When the pads are dry, the interconnections can be drawn in using a ruler (bevel side down). Sharp corners should be avoided as they are a likely cause of subsequent circuit failure.

Fill in the inner radius freehand; otherwise a blob similar to a solder pad can be applied to cover the corner, therefore maintaining a reasonable area of copper adhesion. Examples are shown in Fig. 10. Errors during drawing are removed with a corner of a piece of rag damp with solvent; the dry resist can be chipped away, being careful not to mark the copper surface.

A clean method of applying resist is achieved with plastic film dry transfer sheets, rather like instant lettering. Pad shapes, i.c. clusters and lines are available. The transfer sheet is placed on the copper

Fig. 10. Drawing corners

Sharp bends in the copper tracks of the final board will be weak and could lead to lifting under heat or even fracture. Etching is likely to be unreliable, too. By filling in the corners and tees, or rounding them with the resist pen, this problem can be overcome and a neater appearance result

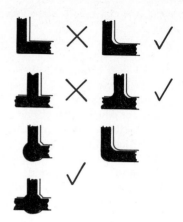

surface and rubbed carefully with a pencil. The transfer adheres to the copper, acting as an effective resist to the etchant. The resist material is fairly thick and must be very carefully rubbed away from the backing sheet to avoid the symbol breaking up. It is important to place a sheet of greaseproof paper between the copper and the rest of the symbols on the sheet to prevent accidental transfer.

A selection of ready prepared stick-on resist symbols from E. R. Nicholls. The resist pattern is rubbed away from the backing like instant lettering

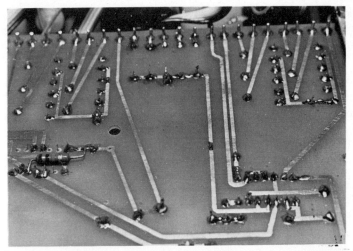

A glass fibre board that has been prepared by marking the circuit pattern with a resist pen, then etched in the usual way

To produce a short line from the long lines that are on the sheet it is recommended that a cut be made in the resist symbol with a razor blade while still on the backing sheet. In this way the line, when rubbed on to the copper, will have a clean end at the correct position.

The sheets of symbols carry a wide range of 'corners' and 'elbows'

The component side of a printed circuit board. Notice the neat layout created by positioning the components in parallel formation

47

and a full selection of ready spaced device pad clusters, which save time and give clean results. After etching, the film shapes are removed by using wire wool, possibly helped by the application of a solvent. The pads have centre holes which indicate the drilling position and act as a centre locator for the drill.

When a number of boards are to be made to the same design, photographic techniques can be used. The process does not call for any specialised items of photographic equipment and it is often quicker to produce a large board photographically than by any of the other methods.

The process consists basically of coating the copper side of the board with photosensitive chemical, which is then held in contact with a transparency of the required pattern and exposed to ultraviolet light. When developed in the usual way, the photo-resist remains

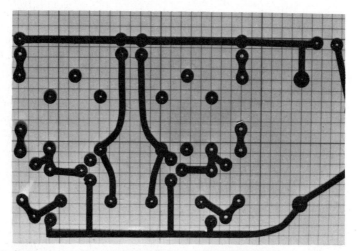

The transparency for photographic p.c.b. production is made by laying down stick-ons on to clear polyester film. For accurate component layout the film is laid over a precision layout grid with 0.1in pitch rulings

on the board covering the copper areas that are required for connections; the board is etched in the usual way. Notes on ultra-violet lamps follow later.

The transparency of the layout pattern is made on polyester or acetate film—a very stable plastic sheet which is 'transparent' to ultraviolet light. The film is laid out over a precision grid which is a sheet of polyester with very accurate rulings on its surface (usually at 0.1 in or 2.5 mm pitch) making up a squared pattern like graph paper. The

48

opaque parts of the layout (where the conductors are to be laid) consist of 'stick-on' symbols. Stick-ons are available both full size and to a larger scale to enable the design to be reduced for greater accuracy. For most purposes, full-size symbols are used to eliminate the need for photographic reduction.

The symbols available cover most types of pads and device connection clusters together with curves and T-junctions. Lines of accurate width are supplied on rolls. All the symbols and lines are self-adhesive and it is only necessary to position them accurately using the layout grid as a reference and press them down. The layout must be done in reverse—as if a 'mirror' image. Use tracing paper to see the design through the back of the drawing. A pair of sharp nosed tweezers, for laying the pads, and a sharp art knife for cutting the end of the lines, are the only tools required.

Stick-ons are available on cards (W. H. Brady and Circuitape) or in roll form (Chartpak) and are simply pressed down into position. Pads and clusters should be laid down first and then the lines introduced to link them. The tape used for lines can be made to turn gentle corners of large radius, but proper corner pieces should be applied for sharp

A collection of clusters and pads and a partly formed basic layout started. (courtesy W. H. Brady Co. Ltd; Chartpak Ltd; P. T. Barclay & partners Ltd.)

bends. The lines should overlap slightly at the top of the pad, but not obscure the central hole which marks the position for the component mounting holes to be drilled in the board.

Copper-clad board can be obtained ready coated with photo-resist and only needs the plastic protective film removed before use. Otherwise, clean board can be sprayed with aerosol photo resist. Obviously, the boards must be kept away from bright light before use. Tungsten lighting has negligible effect on the resist, however, as the ultra-violet content of this light is very small.

Exposure

The stick-on side of the artwork is placed in contact with the resist side of the board and the two placed face upwards on a flat table. To ensure good contact during exposure, a thin sheet of clean glass must be placed on top of the artwork. Glass can absorb ultra-violet light, so it should be as thin and pure as possible; high purity is indicated by the minimum coloration at the clean-cut edge of the glass.

The ultra-violet lamp should be far enough above the board to ensure even light coverage—three feet or one metre away covers approximately one square foot or ten square decimetres. The exposure is then made for a period usually of about four minutes. This has to be found by experiment using small pieces of spare board.

The exposure board is then developed in the developer chemical supplied with the board, or from an aerosol. Very soon the exposed areas of resist will flow away leaving the bare copper to be etched away later. The developed board is dried and left to stand for several minutes while the remaining resist hardens. Then it is ready for etching.

Removal of the resist after etching depends on the type used, but the instructions supplied with the board or aerosol usually recommend a standard solvent such as trichloroethylene or acetone.

The ultra-violet light needed for the exposure of photo-resist needs to be fairly strong. Summer sunlight can be used but the precise exposure times would be unpredictable and rather long (about half an hour).

The lamp depends on a mercury discharge which is strong at the violet end of the spectrum. These lamps need a series ballast inductor to serve as a current limiter, as recommended by the manufacturers, and must never be operated directly from the mains without it (Fig. 11).

Fig. 11. Ultra-violet lamp

The Philips mercury discharge reflector type ultra-violet lamp must be used with a series choke L and a 'power factor' capacitor C to the makers' recommendations

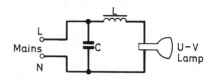

After applying current, a period of about one minute elapses before the output has come up to the full level. This time gives radiation roughly equivalent to 15 seconds at full level and is counted as a quarter of a minute for total exposure.

After switching the lamp off, several minutes have to elapse for the bulb to cool down before it can be switched on again. The problem can be overcome by using ultra-violet tubes that work in an

A reflector type high-pressure mercury discharge ultra-violet lamp and choke for photographic processing (courtesy Philips Electrical Ltd.)

ordinary fluorescent type of circuit. Tubes about two feet (80 cm) long are best for p.c.b. work and at least two tubes are needed to obtain even illumination.

A reflector type of u.v. lamp gives almost a point source of light projecting a very sharp outline of the artwork on to the resist, even if there is a small gap between the two. The artwork and glass plate must be clean, since dust specks cause spots on the finished p.c.b.

Fig. 12. Exposing to u.v. light

The finite thickness of 'stick-on' material means that pads are lifted slightly above the photo resist surface by the conductor strips. Unless the ultra-violet lamp is a point source, or is mounted some distance away, the outline of the pad on the photo resist will not be sharply focused

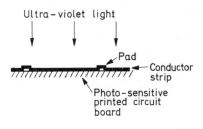

Illumination from ultra-violet tubes is very diffuse and unless the artwork and photo resist are in very close contact, untidy edges are produced. Unfortunately, when using stick-on resist, the artwork does have areas of double thickness of opaque material (Fig. 12). This usually occurs around pads—the result being that the lines are well reproduced but the pads are all rather untidy. This effect is minimised by moving the u.v. lamp further away, but the light intensity is then reduced, and allowance must be made in assessing the required exposure time (Fig. 13).

Fig. 13. Illumination

The illumination on the surface of the photo-sensitive p.c.b. depends on the distance to the u.v. source. The radiated energy from the lamp is spread over a solid angle Φ and the illumination on the surface depends on the portion of the solid angle intercepted by the surface. From the drawing it is evident that, for every doubling of the 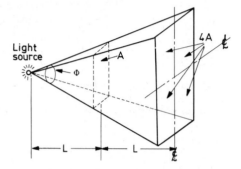 distance from the lamp, the area cut by the solid angle increases four times, reducing the illumination by a factor of four. The effect on exposure is summarised by the inverse law:

$$\text{New exposure} = \text{Old exposure} \times \frac{(\text{new distance})^2}{(\text{old distance})^2}$$

High pressure mercury lamps are being replaced with metal halide lamps in some applications on account of their higher photographic efficiency. The illumination from any lamp follows the inverse square law and this must be borne in mind when changing the distance of the lamp from the photo resist.

Sometimes one can obtain the services of professional processing firms who have precision equipment. One example is the co-ordinatograph which makes a transparency for photographic p.c.b. production by cutting away an opaque film on one side of a clear polyester base. The result is an opaque background with clear film where conductors are required. The cutters used to shave off this opaque film are mounted on a pair of arms whose movement is calibrated in fractions of an inch (or millimetres). It is therefore easy to transfer a design from graph paper on to the scribing film.

The 'Scribemaster' co-ordinatograph produces accurate p.c.b. transparencies for photographic p.c.b. production. The transparencies can be made fairly quickly and are thus inexpensive (courtesy Linton Laboratories Ltd)

The transparency is contact printed on to the photo resist in the same way as a transparency made with stick-ons. If the same photo resist were used for stick-ons the result would be that the conductor areas of the board would be etched away. There are two types of resist—positive and negative working. For use with stick-ons, positive working resist is used, but negative working resist must be used with co-ordinatograph transparencies.

Co-ordinatograph machines are fairly expensive and few amateurs could justify owning one. Often companies who have these machines are prepared to produce a transparency from a drawing for subsequent p.c.b. reproduction by the customer. This is a useful service as the cost of producing a transparency is very reasonable and the boards produced are fully up to professional standards when subsequent processing is carefully carried out.

Etching

The copper foil on the board which is not covered by resist is etched away by a copper dissolving solution. The most common etchant is a solution of ferric chloride which is bought as crystals or lumps from a chemical supplier and dissolved in warm water at the rate of about 300 g to each litre of water. The solution should be kept in a sealed glass bottle or jar. It is very important to handle this chemical with extreme care at all times and not to leave it exposed. The crystals and solution are very messy and corrosive, so should not be handled with bare hands or allowed to come into contact with clothing. Keep it well away from the reach of children and pets. Use protective gloves when processing and mop up all spills immediately with a wet rag.

The solution is a rich brown colour, but with use becomes black and muddy looking. The etchant can be considered exhausted when etching takes too long for completion, or when a black precipitate forms in the storage jar. Since copper is mixed with it during etching, its effects are increasingly impaired; filtering can be carried out to separate the copper.

The board is etched either horizontally or vertically in the solution. For horizontal etching a large, shallow, non-metallic dish is required. A suitable dish to use is a photographer's printing or developing dish, or an old clean glass ovenware dish. It is helpful if it has a small lip moulded in one corner to help when pouring the solution away. The 10 x 8 in (25 x 20 cm) size is adequate for most applications.

Fill the dish to a depth of about ½ in (12 mm) with etchant. The p.c.b. is then laid copper face uppermost on the bottom and agitated by rocking the dish very carefully to disperse the black layer which

Fig. 14. Etching

A tank for vertical etching of p.c.b.s can easily be made from ¼ in (2.5 mm) perspex acrylic sheet. The sides and bottom should be cut to size with very accurate straight and square smooth flat edges. The parts are joined by using Tensol No. 6 cement or liquid chloroform, using butt joints. Setting will take only a few hours; the whole assembly being held in position with rubber bands. By standing the box on a flat sur-

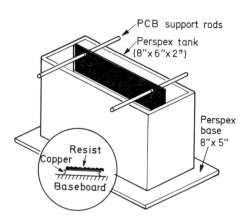

PCB support rods
Perspex tank (8"x6"x2")
Perspex base 8"x5"
Resist
Copper
Baseboard

face, its own weight will be sufficient to hold the box-plate in place. When joined, apply some adhesive around the inside of the joins as a fillet to ensure it being watertight. The copper-clad board can be supported by two crocodile clips soldered to a rod which lays across the top of the tank. Alternatively, two holes can be drilled to accept support rods made from stout perspex or brass as shown. As etching progresses the copper will be seen to dissolve into the liquid; it is important to remove the board as soon as the required amount of etching is finished.

forms on the copper. The speed of etching depends on temperature as well as the thickness of copper and purity of etchant. Etching takes about half an hour at normal room temperature (20°C) and becomes progressively quicker for a warmer solution. The easiest way to warm the solution is to stand the storage bottle in a bowl of hot (not boiling) water before use.

The problem of uneven etching that arises because of the black layer that forms during etching, can be reduced by either floating the board face down, ensuring that there are no air bubbles trapped and the surface clean (processing cannot be watched so easily) or by etching the board vertically (the most satisfactory method); see Fig. 14.

A special tank can be made to etch boards vertically and this has been found to be the best way of producing consistent quality boards. The black layer simply slides down the board and into the bottom of the solution, leaving the board open to the action of the etchant.

Etching is finished when all the copper has been completely dissolved, except that which is protected with resist. The board is immediately removed from the solution, otherwise it is possible for etching to take place under the edges of the resist giving a ragged outline to the pads. The board must be thoroughly washed to remove all traces of etchant and the resist removed by the appropriate method described earlier. Leave to dry in a warm clean atmosphere. A rack suitable for this can be found at home usually, for example a plate rack or mat stand.

Drilling

The etched p.c.b., when washed and stripped of paint, has to be drilled to accept the component leads. If you have followed the advice given earlier, the drilling positions should be clearly seen on the pads; marks exposed to etchant will now be dissolved away leaving the bare board ready to accept the drill. If not then insufficient etching time was allowed.

A number 60 drill (0.040 in or 1 mm) drill is used by convention for all holes at first; if they need to be larger (e.g. for some electrolytics, mounted switches, preset potentiometers or pin tags) the appropriate enlargement size drill can be used afterwards. Use high-speed steel drills in a true-running drill chuck.

The board is always drilled from the copper side to avoid causing burrs on the edges of the holes where the copper has to be soldered. If the drill becomes blunt, the risk of burrs is increased and this will occur more quickly with glass fibre boards. A small 'centre-spot' mark is made to locate the drill for each hole, unless a compass point was used to mark the centre during layout of the resist. Etched drill position marks do not need further preparation for drilling.

The best tools to use for drilling are a hand wheel brace or an electric drill mounted on a drilling pedestal. There are also some light hand held battery operated drills that are designed especially for the job. Using a large or heavy hand-held power drill often results in broken drills. Always clamp the printed circuit board down on to a piece of clean flat wood when drilling.

Sheet s.r.b.p. is built up in layers and unfortunately can chip or flake away on the reverse side as the drill emerges if too much force is

Electric drill mounted in a bench stand. This Black & Decker model can be adjusted to the suitable height above the workpiece

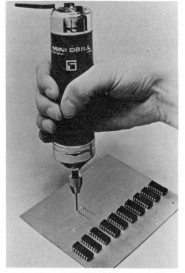

Battery operated drill specially designed for drilling printed circuit boards (courtesy Guest Electronic Distribution Ltd.)

used. Carefully drilled holes look very neat and no finishing or deburring other than a rub with emery cloth to remove the 'whiskers' is needed.

During drilling the copper will probably become fingermarked which will impair soldering, and so the p.c.b. should be cleaned with a hard fibre brush or wire wool. If the p.c.b. is not to be used for a while the cleaned copper can be coated with a flux varnish (PCIOA Multicore Activated Surface Preservative or an aerosol of Philips Protective Coating 815 PCS or Kontact SK10 is recommended).

56

If the board has been left for a while and has not had a preservative coating applied, it may save a lot of trouble if it is polished to remove the tarnish. Once assembled and tested the conductor side of the board can be thinly sprayed with polyurethane from an aerosol to give protection against corrosion of the copper. Commercial boards often have this protection in the form of the solder resist with which the whole board except the solder pads is coated.

Double-sided Layouts

With a single-sided p.c.b. any conductors which cross do so by passing one conductor under a component crossing it. With complex circuits it is not always possible to arrange for crossovers to be effected in this way; therefore a conductor has to be provided on the component side of the board. The simplest way of doing this is to solder a short link wire on the component side of the board.

When a large number of links are needed a double-sided board is usefully employed and large areas of spare copper foil can also be used for screening. Commercial double-sided boards are produced with or without through-hole plating (Fig. 15). A through-hole plated board has a

Fig. 15. Soldering

Through-hole plated p.c.b.s need to be soldered on one side only. Double-sided boards without through-hole plating may require connection between one side and the other, in which case soldering to the component wire must be done on both sides of the board. In cases where the connection must be isolated from the connection on the other side, great care is needed to make sure that solder does not flow through the hole

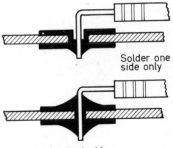

Solder one side only

Solder both sides

tubular layer of copper connecting the two sides of the board through each component hole and only requires the components to be soldered as normal. Where the amateur processes and drills his own board this technique is not readily available without access to special equipment.

A double-sided board without through-hole plating relies on the component leads being soldered on each side of the board to make the necessary connection between the two sides of the board. Accurate registration (alignment) of the etched patterns on the two copper surfaces is very important.

When a resist pen is used the design can be laid down on one side of the board as usual. When dry, the component holes are then drilled. The design for the second side of the board can now be laid down knowing that the registration is correct at the critical component holes where connection between the two sides of the board is made. A similar technique can be used with paint and 'stick-on' resist. Etching of both sides is carried out simultaneously.

Photographic registration is easy to ensure as it is possible to put the designs for the two sides together and visually check that the component holes coincide precisely. The two photographic designs can be taped together to form a sort of envelope into which the sensitised board is slipped for exposure. After one side has been exposed, the board is carefully turned over and the other exposure made. The component holes need only be drilled after etching is complete.

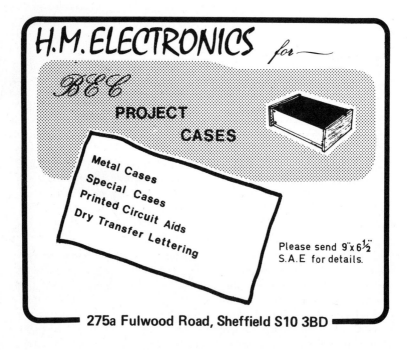

6 Metalwork and cases

In a home electronics workshop it is not always easy or possible to become too involved with case-making metalwork. With a few basic tools, however, it is possible to make chassis and panels, and even to construct simple instrument cases. Constructors with the desire to undertake detailed construction work and design should refer to the Constructor's Guide on *Project Planning and Building*.

The traditional material for electronic metalwork is sheet aluminium which is available in sheets of thickness based on the standard wire gauge (s.w.g.) sizes. The gauge number indicates a sheet thickness the same as the diameter of a wire of the same gauge. For most purposes, 18 s.w.g. (1.2 mm) is quite strong enough for case-making and is easily worked; 16 s.w.g. (1.6 mm) may be necessary for large panels requiring better rigidity under load, and for control panels.

Aluminium sheet is quite an expensive commodity and when one considers the time that is required to fabricate and finish a cabinet it is worth considering the use of a pre-assembled cabinet or kit available. They range from the simple box to elaborate cases formed from complex aluminium extrusions and castings to give prototype equipment a thoroughly professional look.

Complete cabinets are available in either a paint or plastic coated finish or are left as bare metal. Often the front panel is left plain (or covered with a protective sheet of plastic) or has undercoat applied so that the constructor can apply his own choice of finish.

When using a ready-made cabinet the only metalwork involved usually is the drilling of the front panel and the fabrication of some form of chassis or p.c.b. support.

59

Marking Out

It is always advisable to prepare a full-size drawing of a piece of work before cutting so that any planning errors can be rectified on paper with a rubber, rather than after the holes have been made.

Marking out on the job is usually done with reference to two edges (if straight) or reference lines at right angles to each other. A scriber and steel rule are needed for marking out, but with aluminium (especially if coated with protective plastic) a ball point pen used heavily may give clearer lines.

A clear fine line is all that is required to show where cutting, bending and filing is required, but where a hole is to be drilled the centre should be marked out with a centre punch first. This is essential, as otherwise the drill tip will wander away from the intended position.

Cutting and Filing

Straight edges in sheet metal are best cut with a hacksaw (Fig. 16) or hacksaw blade in a pad saw handle, if a guillotine is not available. Tin snips can be used for curved shapes or short cuts; unless used very

Fig. 16. Cutting sheet metal

Sheet metal is easily cut by laying it on the bench, preferably applying clamps, so that the waste part hangs over the edge. If clamps are not available, press firmly with the hand as shown. Use a sharp fine-toothed hacksaw

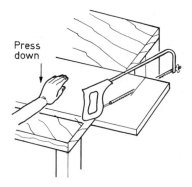

Press down

carefully, a number of small kinks can appear in the cut edge which are difficult to remove except by filing. In any case a small margin of waste (say 1 mm) should be left to allow for filing to the line.

When filing, it is important to file in a direction along the length of the metal (Fig. 17), not across the edge. If possible the work should be held in a vice protected with newspaper, and as low as possible in the jaws. Use a fine toothed file. Soft metals like aluminium can easily clog

60

Fig. 17. Filing metal sheet

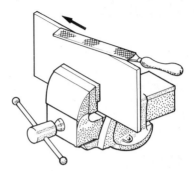

Metal filed in a vice should be supported as near to the edge as possible; paper is inserted to protect the metal surface from biting of the vice jaws. Long, even strokes should be made along the length of the metal (never across it) keeping the file in the same flat plane to ensure a straight clean edge

the teeth of the file. This is known as 'pinning' and is prevented by rubbing chalk into the file before use. The problem is greater with fine files that are used for finishing.

A nibbling tool is very useful for cutting out unusual shapes in sheet metal. This the Adel nibbler from West Hyde Developments Ltd.

Rectangles, squares, ovals and other apertures are easily made in a sheet of soft metal. The outline of the shape is clearly marked and a hole drilled in the centre as large as possible without touching the marked lines. Then, using correctly shaped fine files the hole is gradually

Fig. 18. Cutting square holes

Rectangular holes often need to be made in sheet metal to take slide switches, meters, etc. The hole should be marked clearly (A); drill out as far as possible just short of the line (B). Remove the remainder with a file of the right shape

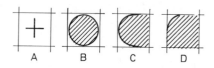

extended to the corners of the marked aperture as shown in Fig. 18.

Pinning can become very troublesome with needle files. The answer is to work slowly without excessive pressure and keep the teeth full of

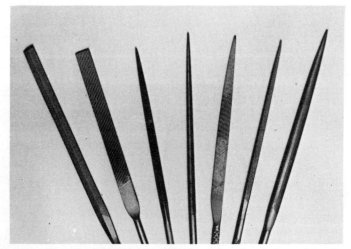

Selection of needle files of various shapes and grades. Left to right: Parallel triangular fine; Flat clean-edge course; Pointed triangular course; Pointed round fine; Knife-edge fine; Pointed half-round fine

chalk. These small files are also useful for enlarging holes or slotting and are called 'Swiss' files or 'rat-tail' files.

Drilling

At some point in the construction of a project, holes need to be drilled. Most materials can be drilled with a twist drill (the normal type of metalwork drill) in either a hand-held wheel brace or an electric drill mounted in a pedestal. High-speed steel drills are always recommended for longer life, even though they are more expensive than ordinary carbon drills.

When mounted in a vertical drill stand, an electric drill is very easy to use and all holes should be drilled accurately and square to the surface of the sheet. The work is held with a metal worker's (or tool-maker's) vice or clamped down with G-clamps or similar to the table. Always place a smooth clean piece of waste wood under the work-piece to protect the drill bit when it penetrates right through. It will also absorb vibration during drilling and ensure a clean breakthrough of the drill—otherwise a rough burr can result. *It is dangerous to hold the workpiece by hand during drilling*.

Using a hand drill, the work must be held in a vice, protected from the marking of the vice jaws with sheets of newspaper or rag. To prevent distortion of the work while drilling, the punched hole centre should be as near to the vice jaws as possible—allowing room for the drill chuck, of course.

Large holes (say over ¼ in) should always be preceded with a smaller pilot hole. This is necessary because the tip of the drill has a small flat non-cutting edge and can wander unless the drill is firmly guided.

Bending

Aluminium, brass and tinplate are the easiest metals that can be bent in a vice without special equipment. Results are rarely as good as can be obtained with the proper bending machine, but with a little practice a

Fig. 19. Bending metal sheet

These diagrams show the se-quence of bending metal sheet by hand. The metal is held between two pieces of angle iron in a vice, so that the fold line is accurately positioned along the edge of the angle corner. Insert newspaper between the metal sheet and the angle iron for protection. Use a piece of wood to push the metal over, directing the force at the fold mark to obtain the sharpest bend. Finally tap the surface using the wood and a light ham-mer to improve the corner of the bend and to flatten the rest of the sheet. Never hit the metal sheet with a bare hammer head

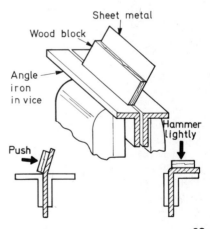

63

satisfactory job can be done. The line of the bend should be marked to coincide with the inside corner. Fig. 19 should be studied with the following instructions.

Sheet metal is gripped in a vice or clamped to the bench between strips of strong aluminium or (better still) steel angle section that is accurately aligned with the bend mark. The tops of the pieces of angle must correspond exactly. The work is placed between the angle strips and the vice tightened so that the fold line is just on the corner of the piece of angle. The metal is then bent by pushing very firmly with a flat piece of wood along the entire length of bend, the force being concentrated at the point of bending. The metal should be pushed firmly onto the face of the angle and then allowed to spring back naturally—pushing too hard will put a bend at the limit of the upper face of the angle.

The fold will usually end up about 5° short of a right-angle and this last amount of bending is done by holding a piece of wood over the bend and hitting it firmly with a hammer along its length. If this is

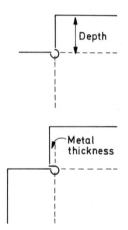

Fig. 20. Corners

A hole drilled in the corners of a chassis before bending prevents the formation of a mis-shapen corner and helps to achieve a straight bend where needed

By allowing a slightly excess amount of metal on one of the cut edges, a neat overlapping corner can be obtained. The extra allowance should be equal to the metal thickness

overdone the metal will fatigue and become thin at the fold. At worse, particularly with brass, it can fracture. The secret is to be firm but careful—brute force will not do!

When removed from the vice, the fold should be clean and sharp. A small amount of surplus metal may spill over and make the sheet slightly wider at the bend, but this is easily filed away.

When two folds are made perpendicular to each other, as for example in the folding of aluminium to make a box, a difficulty arises in that the metal at the apex of the corner squeezes out of line. This can be remedied by drilling a hole, of diameter roughly equal to the metal thickness (Fig. 20), at the intersection of the two bending lines before the redundant square of metal in the corner of the sheet is cut away. Accurate bending will thus be easier to achieve. To make a neat corner an extra thickness of metal should be left on one of the sides which overlaps the edge of the other side. Obviously the edges must be filed smooth before bending.

P.C.B. Mounting

Usually most of the components for a project are contained on a form of wiring board, be it Veroboard, matrix board or a printed circuit board. These panels have to be supported within the cabinet in such a

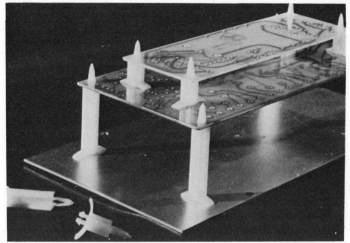

Insulated p.c.b. pillars made from nylon. These are a push-fit into the drilled holes and facilitate stacked board mounting. They are available from several suppliers

way as to offer the boards the full protection of the cabinet whilst in no way impairing their normal operation. Any strain imposed on the board by virtue of weighty components or inadequate support will usually result in fractured copper foil or loosened solder joints.

It is usual to mount boards so that the component side is accessible —it is then possible to adjust preset controls and measure voltages on component leads without having to refer to the wiring layout. A clearance of at least 3/16 in (5 mm) is left behind the board so that protruding component leads do not contact the metalwork, which is usually earthed to screen the whole instrument.

Several commercial insulating board supports are available or insulated pillars or 6BA bolts can be used with three nuts (Fig. 21). An insulating

Fig. 21. Mounting p.c.b.s

Printed circuit boards can be easily supported using ready made nylon pillars as shown in the photograph, or by mounting on 6BA bolts using the adjustable nut facility to clamp soldering tags and make earthing connections, using a shakeproof washer

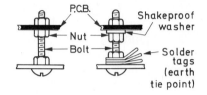

support can be positioned anywhere on a clear area of the board unless it is decided to use one of the supports as the earthing connection from the board. In this case only one such earthing point should be made (otherwise multiple earth troubles may appear) and a shakeproof washer must be used on the copper side to 'bite' through any oxidation and make good electrical contact. The main earth tie point solder tags can be fitted to this bolt. This method of construction is quite neat and is used commercially. If the board is to be operated loose from its mountings for tests or fault-finding, this connection must be made good.

Adhesives

Adhesives are useful in construction for securing large components and holding display components in position. Impact adhesives such as Evo-stik are thinly coated onto each surface, left until almost dry (15 minutes) and the parts are then pressed together. Providing that the surfaces are clean the bond is very strong. These adhesives are used to secure veneers to cabinets and can be used to seal drive cord knots, or hold connecting wires in place where other clips are too clumsy.

The epoxy resin adhesives, such as Araldite, are capable of strong bonds on most surfaces, including metal and glass. They are mixed from the contents of two tubes, the most common error being to use far too much for the job in hand. Epoxies are capable of limited gap filling if the surfaces are not smooth but they should be clean and dry. Quick setting epoxies are available that have achieved useful strength after just a few minutes. Always follow the manufacturer's instructions carefully for best results.

These adhesives are permanent and removal is almost impossible once set so make sure that your procedures are correct. Do not allow epoxy adhesives to come in contact with clothing or the skin. Use a small screwdriver for mixing on a piece of glass and wipe off surplus with newspaper or rag immediately.

The strongest adhesives generally available at present are from the cyanoacrylate family and produce exceptional bonds on contact, except on some plastics and porous surfaces. They are not capable of gap filling so surfaces should be clean, flat and smooth. Acetone is a recommended surface cleaner. 'Cyanolit' is a typical cyanoacrylate.

Heatsinks

Semiconductor devices handling relatively high current often needs to be mounted on a metal heatsink.

To keep the thermal resistance to a minimum the area of contact between the heatsink and the device must be as large as possible. Maximum heat transfer is achieved by using silicone grease (with zinc oxide additive) as a contact paste between the two. Obviously any holes that have to be drilled should be as small as possible to preserve the contact surface and burrs must be completely removed.

Selection of large and small transistor heat sinks, including a rather novel 'glue-on' clip for DIL packages (courtesy Redpoint Ltd., Doram Electronics Ltd.)

Black anodised U clip for TO-3 transistor package

Many of these devices have their case connected to the collector or other electrode so when a number of devices are mounted on one heatsink they must all be insulated. This is achieved by inserting a thin

Push-on clips for cooling TO-5 transistor packages

mica washer coated with silicone grease between the transistor and the heat sink (Fig. 22). The mounting screws are insulated from the heat-sink using specially moulded plastic bushes. The mounting holes in

Fig. 22. Mounting power transistors

Metal cased power transistors are mounted on heat sinks to assist with heat dissipation. The transistor case is often connected to an electrode, so an insulating mounting kit should be used with it. The holes for the mounting bolts are drilled slightly oversize to accommodate the nylon nut insulator. All holes must be deburred to avoid damaging the mica washer. Efficiency of cooling is improved by applying silicone grease before screwing down firmly

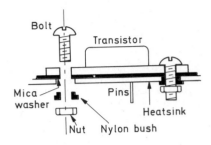

the heat sink have to be made large enough to accommodate these bushes which may have a surface shoulder on which the nut is fitted. Alternatively, nylon nuts and bolts can be used. Details on drilling for heatsink transistors are given in manufacturers' data. Two examples are shown for the popular TO3 and TO66 cases in Fig. 23.

Fig. 23. Drilling for power transistors

Recommended drilling details for standard TO66 and TO3 metal cased transistors. All holes are drilled to 4 mm diameter or using a No. 22 drill

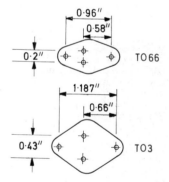

All holes drilled in the heatsink must be smooth and slightly countersunk. It is always advisable to check the transistor/heatsink insulation with a meter prior to wiring up. Thermally damaged transistors can be expensive to replace.

To improve the dissipation of heat from the heatsink into the surrounding air, fins are usually made an integral part of the heatsink design. In order not to impede the rising flow of warm air heat sinks

69

must be mounted with the fins in a vertical plane otherwise efficiency suffers.

Large thyristors and diodes come in 'stud mounting' packages (Fig. 24). The construction is similar to that of a large bolt and the

TO-3 packages mounted on an extruded aluminium heatsink designed for mounting on a printed circuit board

Large finned heatsink with fins on both sides to dissipate heat from high power transistors (courtesy Redpoint Ltd.)

A plastic package power transistor mounted with a mica insulating kit on a matt black heatsink

Fig. 24. Mounting thyristors

Stud mounted thyristors and diodes do not usually dissipate very high power and can be cooled by a simple U heat sink. If devices do not share the sink no insulating kit is required. Matt black anodised heat sinks are available commercially or can be simply made from 16 s.w.g. (1.6 mm) aluminium or copper; a matt black finish will assist heat radiation, but should only be a very thin coating as its thermal conductivity is very low

device is secured to the heatsink with a nut and washer. Usually the case is connected to one electrode so care must be taken to use an insulated mounting kit if a number of devices are to share the same metal heat sink.

7 Presentation and finishing

Cabinets and panels are painted to improve their appearance and make the completed project attractive and hardwaring. To preclude the possibility of marking the newly painted metalwork, as many holes and cut-outs as possible should be made before painting. It is always best to paint before fitting components.

Before any paint can be applied to the metal surface it has to be cleaned and smoothed with wire wool, which also 'keys' the surface a little. All traces of grease must be removed with a rag soaked in a suitable solvent.

Most metals benefit by being primed before the first coat of paint is applied. Metal primer or aluminium paint helps to prevent the paint flaking away from the metal surface. It can be sprayed but is more effective if brushed on and smoothed with very fine emery paper to remove the brush marks.

With skill and the correct consistency of paint, metalwork can be well painted by hand. Good results are obtained more easily, however, by spraying. If brush painting, never apply one coat until the previous one is thoroughly set, and do not apply thick coatings.

Aerosols are available containing quick drying cellulose paints as well as standard slow enamels in both gloss and 'silk' finishes. Cellulose paints have the considerable advantage of fast drying which allows rapid recoating, but the slower enamels do seem to give a much deeper gloss that is less easily scratched. Never apply cellulose paint on a previously enamel coated surface and *vice versa* or blistering will occur.

Spray guns are very much cheaper to use than aerosols and offer the constructor the possibility of using any type of paint or finish, as well as mixing special colours. Modern modelmaker's spray guns are powered from a renewable cylinder of propellant and will hold just a small quantity of paint if necessary—reducing wastage on small jobs.

When using either a spray gun or an aerosol, the paint must be applied in very thin layers otherwise the finish may be patchy or show run marks. Successive coats can be sprayed on while the surface is still tacky or after it has fully hardened and been rubbed down with emery paper to remove irregularities and provide a 'key' for the next coat. If spraying has to be carried out in the workshop or garage (paints are toxic and must not be used in the kitchen) it is essential to cover valuable items with newspaper otherwise the mist of the paint will settle and spoil them. Best results are usually obtained in a warm temperature (about 20°C or more) so that the paint will 'flow' and give a good gloss.

Selection of case designs to suit a variety of projects, from West Hyde Developments Ltd.

Industrial equipment is often treated with a 'hammer finish' paint. A 'one tin' paint is available in many colours to produce this kind of finish on all surfaces and is suitable for brushing or spraying. It is a cellulose paint made from two immiscible colours which are applied together and separate on the surface resulting in a very rugged mottled effect that hides quite large scratches and marks on the metal—it is ideal for castings and die cast boxes. See the photograph later in this chapter.

Best results from hammer finish paints are obtained only if the tin of paint or the reservoir of the spray gun are agitated to keep the two components mixed. A thick coating applied quickly gives the best pattern and does not show brush marks. The paint does not usually run if applied correctly, but keep the workpiece horizontal if possible.

Range of cases made from mild steel and enamel finished in plain, 'crackle', or 'hammer' finish. These examples from Arbour are well suited to rugged use, such as test instruments

The finish is resilient and moisture repellent making it suitable for instruments or projects that have to withstand a severe environment such as motor car accessories or outdoor gadgets.

Brushed Aluminium

An attractive and professional finish for home equipment is 'brushed aluminium', as found on some commercial audio equipment. This rather plush finish is easily applied to a sheet of aluminium but it is important that the surface is not deeply marked otherwise the marks will show through. It is not, as one might expect, a kind of paint; it is a treatment applied to bare aluminium panels that are in good condition. They can be subsequently coated with clear polyurethane spray lacquer to protect the surface so treated.

The aluminium sheet needs to be firmly supported, possibly by a piece of double-sided adhesive tape, on a pile of newspaper. A good squirt of oil is spread over the surface and brushing carried out by applying firm long strokes using a wire brush or wire wool for a finer finish. The brush should be moving before contacting the metal other-

74

wise the ends will take on a different finish. Plenty of oil should be applied to prevent the surface 'pulling', and becoming white, crystalline and rough. A good finish is achieved fairly quickly and an idea of progress gauged by wiping the oil off with a rag. It is a good idea to experiment first with a piece of scrap aluminium to assess the treatment.

The brushed panel is cleaned with trichloroethylene to remove all traces of the oil and then sprayed with a light coat of polyurethane as soon as possible to maintain the bright 'silky' look. Lettering can be applied as if it were an ordinary painted panel (or before the polyurethane is applied if using dry transfers).

Holes should be drilled in the panel before 'brushing' as smooth slightly rounded edges are formed during brushing. Too much pressure when brushing a panel with holes drilled results in streaks which are difficult to remove once they have formed.

Front Panel Layout

A great deal of thought precedes the final layout of commercial equipment from the aspect of user convenience, and certain conventions have grown over the years—the most obvious one being that the clockwise rotation of a control is to bring about an increase in the variable being controlled.

Controls should be grouped logically so that associated functions are all controlled from the same region of the panel.

Indicators (meters and c.r.t.s) are usually placed at the top left of an instrument so that a right-handed operator does not obscure the display while making adjustments.

Domestic equipment, such as hi-fi gear or home gadgets, has to be aesthetically pleasing and often does not have a great many controls. The layout of the panel is usually suggested by the function of the unit and a good guide can be obtained from commercial counterparts. It is tempting to cover domestic equipment with knobs and switches, resulting in a versatile unit, but this is always a grave mistake. Simplicity of operation is reflected in an elegantly simple front panel which blends well with non-technical domestic settings. Additional controls can be hidden beneath a hinged flap or fitted to the back of unit if not required for everyday operation.

Thinking more along the lines of test equipment, operation of complicated instruments is far easier if the controls are not only grouped together but are actually linked in some way to show the dependence of one control upon another or to follow logical association when

75

operating in sequence. The least ambiguous way of providing these links is with fine black lines on the panel. These also save unnecessary panel writing which is time consuming during construction and confusing in operation. Panel marking and labels should be applied before fitting components otherwise knobs and spindles will get in the way.

Sheets of black lines suitable for panel marking are available as rub-on dry transfer sheets. To achieve a line with a clean break at the required point it is recommended that the line be slightly scribed through with a knife at the end point while still on the dry transfer sheet. The line will then release with a clean, well defined end.

As an alternative, lines can be drawn with waterproof (spirit based) fibre tip pens. Very few pens seem to be available with a suitable fine point but the Pentel 50M and N50 pens are suitable. The solvent in the pens may try to soften the surface of freshly applied cellulose paint and, in this case, the work should be put somewhere warm to harden; less pressure should be applied when the line is redrawn.

Ready made control labels available in transfer form provide a neat finished appearance to panels. These are among the various items of hardware provided by Ramar Constructor Services. An example of hammer finish paint is shown on the diecast box lid

Neat, well laid out lettering gives any project a professional image and puts the finishing touch to all the hard work. Some form of prepared letters or even complete words are used and there are several methods available.

Embossed tapes can be applied with the desired letters as selected on the dial of a simple hand held machine. The letters appear near white and the background can be chosen to blend with the colour of the panel or to complement it. Very neat layouts are obtained if the words are cut from the tape using a sharp knife (scissors leave a white

76

Embossed labels show up clearly where quick reference to switch positions is needed. These were produced by the constructor with a 'Dymo' label maker

edge) and are arranged to be exactly central on the strip of tape.

Adhesion of these tapes onto painted surfaces can weaken after a time unless the panel is quite warm when the strip is applied; if it is too hot, the plastic will soften and the letters will be spoilt.

Several companies offer sheets of self-adhesive common electronics labels such as 'Volume', 'Input', 'Amplifier'. Abbreviations and symbols are included on most sheets. Both coloured and transparent back-

Selection of self-adhesive scales and dry transfer labels in black and white (courtesy Data Publications Ltd., Letraset Inc.)

grounds are available and the required word is simply cut out neatly with sharp scissors or a knife and stuck to the panel. The lettering is fairly durable but can be improved by spraying with clear lacquer.

Dry transfer sheets offer the neatest appearance when well applied, being available in a wide range of sizes and styles. The words are made up letter by letter, ensuring accurate alignment by using the guide marks on the sheet. Always use fairly new sheets; old sheets that have been stored tend to become dirty and the plastic film characters brittle.

The letter or symbol is released from the support sheet by simply pressing the symbol against the panel and lightly rubbing the sheet over the letter with a pencil or ball pen. Be careful not to allow adjacent characters to be applied; in any case mistakes are easily corrected by removing with a sharp knife and applying a new character. One way to protect the panel from the erroneous transfer of other characters is to fix a sheet of paper so that the top edge can also act as a straight line guide for the alignment of the applied lettering (Fig. 25).

Fig. 25. Lettering

When applying dry transfer lettering, place the panel on the table, holding it in place with adhesive tape. Fix the transparent backing sheet down on the panel, using adhesive tape, so that the top edge can be used as a straight edge to rub down the lettering in line. It will also protect the panel from sticky hands and unwanted transfers. Always space the lettering evenly from the position of the word centre allowing for variations in letter width in determining the centre

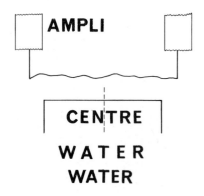

Complete electronic words and abbreviations such as μF, MHz, V, ±, etc are available on some of the specialist sheets. By making each word from individual letters, it is possible to mix letter heights to give such expressions as h_{FE}. Letters with serifs (ornate points or flares) should be avoided as the serifs are more difficult to transfer. A simple style of plain lettering is much better and produces a neater appearance.

Time and patience is required to hand-draw a scale on paper, which is then stuck to the panel. Fortunately, ready prepared scales are now available both on clear self-adhesive film and on dry transfer sheets and are intended for rescaling meters as well as panels. The scale numbers and lettering can be added using one of the aforementioned techniques.

78

Perspiration moisture from the fingers and scuffing from finger nails can mar the appearance of lettering on a control panel, so some form of protection is advisable, such as a spray coating on the panel. When spraying any panel, or lettering, the very thinnest possible layer should be applied otherwise problems can arise. Sometimes the lacquer solvent softens the paint already on the panel, which colours the lacquer, obliterating some of the lettering. The solvent may also dissolve the ink from felt tip line pens. This is of no consequence unless the coating of lacquer is fairly thick when the ink from the line diffuses into the layer of lacquer, giving a fuzzy outline. A flood of lacquer can also dislodge poorly affixed characters. It is always worthwhile in the long run to experiment first on a spare piece of aluminium or appropriate surface.

Leave the finished panel overnight in a warm clean atmosphere to set. When thoroughly set dry, the panel is now ready for the controls to be mounted and suitable knobs fitted.

Equipment to be used domestically can easily be built into a wooden 'sleeve' which goes a long way to taking away the harsh metal-box

A wooden sleeve case designed for this home made project for use in the home

appearance. Solid wood is difficult to use and expensive so the basic shell is made up from veneered plywood. Veneers are now commonly available at most d.i.y. shops.

The simplest wooden sleeve is easily made from four pieces of ply glued and pinned together to form a box (Fig. 26). It can be veneered on the four sides and the front rim, leaving a surround of wood. With a little skill the panel can be inset a little from the front edge of the wood, but veneer must be applied to the inside face of the sleeve at the front, and allowance must be made for this in establishing the case dimensions.

Fig. 26. Wooden case (1)

This simple wooden sleeve is made from four lengths of plywood, pinned and glued or screwed tightly together. Apply a suitable veneer or laminate to the top and sides before the front edges. Mitre the corners if possible to obtain the best finish

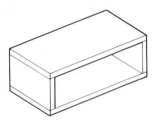

A particularly attractive form of sleeve is made by covering the electronics with a neatly veneered wooden top, the same width as the front panel, and enclosing the whole between two veneered 'cheeks'

This pleasing cabinet is an example of how a simple 'book-end' case can make a project look attractice without complications. The case was produced by H. M. Electronics and the front panel by Ramar Constructor Services

(Fig. 27). A narrow strip of veneered ply can be screwed to the underside of the chassis to show underneath the front panel to complete the 'framing'. Any parts of the unit needing access must be arranged in the design.

The veneers are easily applied using a thin contact adhesive and are trimmed to size with a sharp knife or small plane. The overlap of veneers on corners should be such as to be unseen from the front. A durable finish can be obtained by applying very thin coats of clear lacquer on a clean cloth—rubbing well into the grain. Several coats will probably be needed. Proprietary wood finishes or french polish treatment is easily applied.

Fig. 27. Wooden case (2)

This alternative case is easy to make and constitutes two side cheeks and a top cover with a bottom brace. The front panel can be recessed to great effect. When doing so remember to veneer the inside of parts A before assembly as well as the front and top of part B. Assemble with pins and glue or screws and complete the veneer. Also veneer the top and front of part C

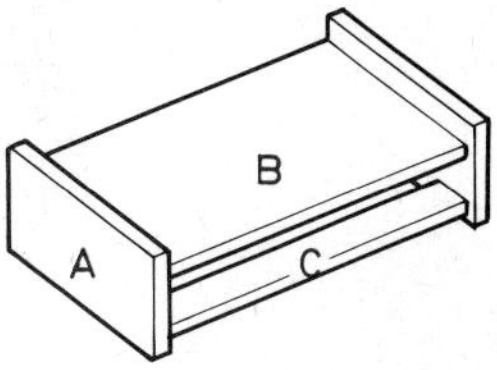

To finish off the cabinet either small rubber feet or self-adhesive draught excluder are fitted to the underside to protect the surface on which the equipment stands.

8 Testing and fault finding

Constructors should not despair should a project fail to work as expected. Even in a complex electronic assembly the chances of a mistake are fairly high, even for a skilled constructor. One learns with experience to treat fault-finding as an integral part of construction.

Most faults will be found to be constructional errors and are located simply by carefully checking the drawings against the model. A routine check before switching on will possibly reveal several faults and save damaging components by applying power in a fault condition. Common constructional errors are:

Wrong resistors or capacitors (misread colour codes),
Incorrect transistor connections or types,
Veroboard conductors not broken when required,
Switch wiring transposed or incorrectly interpreted,
Poor soldering, or simple missed connections.

Should no obvious construction error be found then one must resort to conventional test techniques to reveal the trouble. At this stage it is worth re-reading the circuit description to gain a full understanding of how the project should work.

Without a test meter the electronics engineer is virtually blind. Apart from a soldering iron and cutters it is probably the most important item in any workshop.

The multimeter (or volt-ohm-meter—VOM) as its name suggests has facilities for measuring a wide range of d.c. voltage, d.c. current, resistance, a.c. voltage and sometimes a.c. current as well. A few meters also offer very useful capacitance ranges. The accuracy of almost all the meters available (within 3 or 4%) is adequate for basic testing

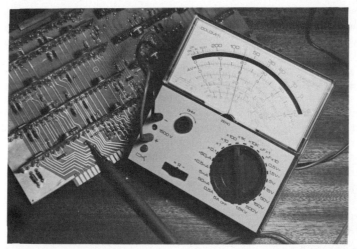

Using a multimeter to measure the d.c. resistance and continuity of part of a circuit board withdrawn from its housing. This instrument typifies the large clear scale and anti-parallax mirror (courtesy Chinaglia (UK) Ltd.)

purposes and is clearly better with a large open scale. The most important feature of the multimeter is its sensitivity, as it will determine what effect the meter resistance will have on the circuit being tested and

Fig. 28. Using a multimeter to measure voltage

A 10 kΩ/V voltmeter passes a current of 100 μA when full-scale deflection of the pointer occurs. A current of 90 μA will pass when measuring 9 V on the 10 V range. The same meter will indicate only 6 V instead of the correct figure of 9 V when measuring the base voltage of the emitter follower; the two 100 kΩ resistors are a simple voltage divider. The discrepancy is due to internal resistance of the meter, which is 100 kΩ on the 10 V range, reducing the effective resistance from base to ground to only 50 kΩ. This effect can be reduced by using a meter of higher kΩ/V or even an electronic voltmeter with an input resistance greater than 1 MΩ

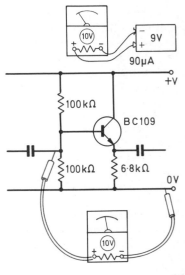

83

could result is misleading interpretation of the values being measured.

The resistance of a voltmeter is quoted in kilohms per volt. Thus a 10 kΩ/V meter on the 15 V range would have a resistance of 150 kΩ, sufficiently high not to affect most transistor circuits (Fig. 28). Generally, 10 kΩ/V is the minimum sensitivity that can be tolerated and 20 kΩ/V is far more usual. The rectifier arrangements of most meters give a much reduced sensitivity on the a.c. ranges (lower kΩ/V) but some more recent meters are rather more sensitive, for example, 20 kΩ/V on both d.c. and a.c., or even as high as 50 kΩ/V.

With a multimeter to measure d.c. voltages it is surprising how quickly a fault can be isolated. Currents are rarely measured directly (except for total supply current) because this means breaking a conductor, which is not always easy. The total current flowing through a resistor is easily found by measuring the voltage across its ends and applying Ohm's law. The d.c. current is equal to the voltage across it divided by the resistance (see Fig. 29).

Fig. 29. Using a multimeter to measure current

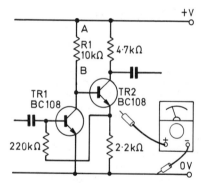

The current through R1 is easily found by measuring the voltage at point A and point B and their difference by the value of the resistor. A correction can be made for the current in the voltmeter if significant.

Using a 10 kΩ/V meter on the 10 V range, the voltage at A is found to be 10 V and at B 4 V. The current flowing in R1 is then

$$\frac{10 - 4}{10\ 000} \quad A = 600\ \mu A$$

At a reading of 6/10 of full scale, the meter current would be 60 μA (100 μA at f.s.d.) so the resistor current is 600 − 60 = 540 μA

The transistor does most of the effective work in each stage of a piece of equipment and voltage checks on the three terminals usually indicate pretty conclusively if that stage is functioning correctly (Fig. 30).

The voltage between emitter and base of a silicon transistor when biased for amplification (as opposed to switching) is always about 0.7 V (0.3 V for germanium). A voltage much higher than this indicates an excessive base current while a voltage of less than 0.4 V

84

(0.15 V germanium) means that the transistor is 'cut off', or passing no collector current.

Fig. 30. Transistor currents and voltages

The base-emitter voltage of a silicon transistor (V_{be}) is always 0.7 V in normal operation; 0.3 V for germanium. The small base current I_b is multiplied by the gain of the transistor (h_{fe}) to give the collector current I_c. The emitter current I_e is equal to $I_c + I_b$ but, as I_b is so small, I_e and I_c are considered as being virtually equal. When the base voltage is fixed by the potential divider R1 and R2, then the emitter voltage must be 0.7 V less than V_b. Therefore, I_e is governed by R_E

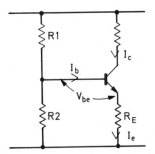

The collector current is almost equal to the emitter current so if the base voltage is fixed by a voltage divider network (as is usual), varying the emitter resistor will only vary the emitter and collector current because the emitter voltage must be 0.7 V less than that on the base.

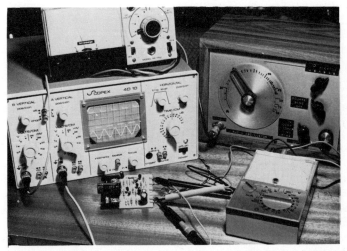

A well laid out test bench and a specimen under test. Little space is needed for basic instruments such as these. Left to right: Scopex 4D10 oscilloscope; Heath-kit electronic voltmeter (also shown in kit form earlier); Home made audio oscillator with sine and square wave output; Iskra multimeter

85

If the collector is the output terminal of the amplifier, it should operate at about half the supply voltage; for an emitter follower the emitter voltage should be about half the supply voltage (and obviously the base 0.7 V higher). These conditions may not be met exactly for practical reasons but collectors that are almost at full supply voltage or zero in a non-switching circuit can mean that there is a fault in that stage. A common construction fault is to transpose the two base bias divider resistors, causing a large collector current and high emitter voltage with a low collector voltage. If the collector is within a volt of the emitter then the transistor is quite likely 'saturated' and cannot amplify.

Direct-coupled amplifier circuits usually derive their operating point from a single voltage divider across the supply lines and any errors are obviously amplified through the system leading to widely incorrect operating conditions.

Audio power amplifiers are mostly designed as high powered d.c. amplifiers; operating voltage errors can be destructive to the output devices. A limiting resistor, such as a bulb of appropriate voltage, both protects the circuit and gives a visual indication of excess current conditions.

Voltage measurement must be a logical process which centres on the circuitry surrounding an obvious error. Often in newly built equipment voltage checks reveal incorrect transistor/diode (see Constructors Guide on *Electronic Components*), faulty components (damaged when forming the leads?) or incorrect wiring, although this should have been traced earlier.

Sometimes incorrect voltages in a stage do not appear to be caused by any construction fault and suspicion rests on the transistor itself. A proper transistor tester (several kits are available) makes short work of analysing a device but an indication of the state of the device can be obtained from the ohms range of a multimeter. To do this means carefully removing the transistor from its mounting position, making a note of the connection details. Fig. 31 shows how to check transistors and diodes with a multimeter.

A transistor can be considered as two diodes connected back to back and a failure of the device often shows as a failure of one of the diodes which can easily be checked with an ohmmeter (remembering that in the 'ohms' position current flows out of the black test lead which is therefore positive with respect of the red terminal).

An indication of current gain or leakage can also be obtained with an ohmmeter but results depend very much on the particular meter used, as a wide range of internal voltages are used and the test currents vary so much. Fig. 31b shows a simple means of checking the leakage current of electrolytic capacitors.

While the meter tells a lot about the static characteristics of a circuit, its spread of response is too slow to enable dynamic or alternating current to be followed. While the a.c. ranges allow an alternating signal to be measured, no information about frequency or wave shape can be gained.

Fig. 31. Checking components with a multimeter

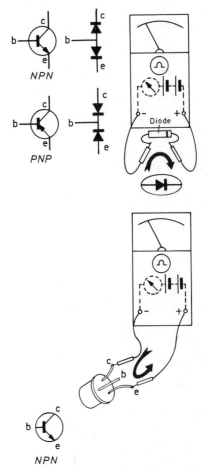

Transistors resemble two diodes in back-to-back formation, with the common connection representing the base terminal. The two diodes can be checked with a low voltage ohmmeter as shown, although this cannot be taken as a conclusive test, but will indicate total junction breakdown. The ohmmeter has an internal battery to provide the voltage reference on the dial in terms of the resistance across the terminals. The positive terminal of the battery is connected to the negative terminal of the instrument. The pointer will show near full scale deflection when the red (+) terminal of the test meter is connected to the cathode (+) end of the diode and the black (−) of the test meter to the anode end of the diode.

Transistor gain can be roughly checked by connecting the test-meter to the emitter and collector, so that normal operating current flow is possible; black (−) to collector of an npn type, red (+) to the collector of a pnp type. Connecting the base to the collector should give a low resistance reading, while connecting the base to the emitter should increase the leakage resistance to a high value. Germanium devices have a poor leakage even when up to specification. The range between the low resistance and high resistance states is roughly indicative of the current gain—the wider the range the better. The technique can be modified by connecting a 1 MΩ resistor from collector to base, the meter reading roughly indicating the gain on the resistance scale, the gain being the number of times that the resistance reading can be divided into 1 000 000.

87

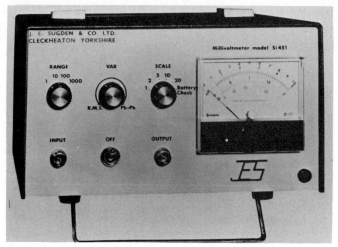

A basic electronic millivoltmeter from J. E. Sugden & Co Ltd. with a unique set of ranges in a 1, 2, 5, 10 sequence and range multiplers

Fig. 31b. Testing components

This simple circuit tests the leakage of electrolytic capacitors. A dead short will be shown by full scale deflection. After the capacitor has had time to charge, the meter should settle at a reading of less than 50 μA for capacitors of less than 500 μF; higher for larger types.

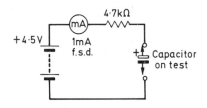

An oscilloscope gives a visual representation of voltage with respect to time and is the only way of actually observing the dynamic response of a circuit. When calibrated, an oscilloscope can measure both voltage and time thus enabling the frequency of the signal to be measured as

Fig. 32. Sine wave

An oscilloscope display of a sine wave. The vertical scale represents 10 V per division; the horizontal scale (time) 10 μs per division. On many oscilloscopes 1 division equals 1 cm. The r.m.s. voltage is 0.707 of the peak value, in this case 10.605 V. Frequency is equal to 1/80 μs or 12500 Hz.

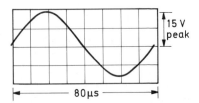

well as its amplitude. Of course, a graphical representation is displayed on the screen (Fig. 32).

There is always a restriction on the maximum frequency which can be accurately displayed on an oscilloscope. Cheaper scopes have a useful response up to about 1 MHz enabling most audio conditions to be monitored, while the more expensive types, more often found in industry, are suitable for use with radio, television, radar, and high speed switching circuits.

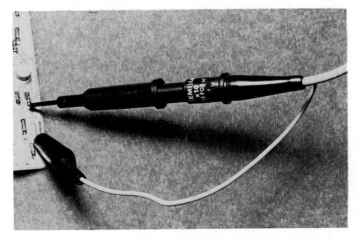

An oscilloscope probe for ÷ 1 and ÷ 10 extension of the input. This is the EMI probe. Probes of this kind are available as 'probe kits' with ancillary connectors and trimming tool

Present day technology has enabled a few companies to produce scopes of versatile performance, for basic experimental work and fault finding, but without the super refinements that are more appropriate to specialist applications. These can be usefully employed on most domestic entertainment equipment.

The input impedance of scopes is generally 1 MΩ which is sufficiently high not to upset most circuits. However, at high frequencies the reactance of the self-capacitance in the screened connecting lead (say a few hundred pF) becomes so low as to greatly affect circuit operation. By using a 10:1 probe the scope input impedance is raised to 10 MΩ with a capacitance of around 15 pF (Fig. 33). The penalty for the improvement is that the attenuation of ÷10 has to be corrected by using higher gain setting on the scope. Sufficient gain may not then be present to allow the investigation of very small signals. Straight through or ÷1 probes are available to give no reduction in gain while

89

still keeping the capacitance to a minimum, usually less than 50 pF—certainly better than using a length of co-ax as the input lead. Combination ÷1/÷10 probes are also available.

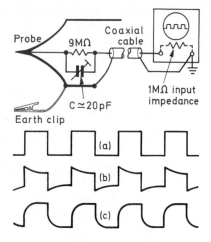

Fig. 33. Oscilloscope probe

To increase the input impedance of a scope to 10 MΩ, and reduce the tip capacitance to less than 20 pF, a ÷ 10 probe is used. The capacitor C is adjusted to give good fidelity of a 1 kHz square wave (a).

    (a) correctly adjusted probe;
    (b) capacitor set too high;
    (c) capacitor set too low, attenuating high frequencies.

Any form of attenuator probe has to be adjusted for optimum fidelity of a 1 kHz square wave display, otherwise the frequency response of the scope will no longer be flat and frequency errors will be introduced.

For testing and fault-finding circuits involving amplifiers a suitable signal must be used. Sometimes signals are present in the equipment (e.g. an electronic organ) but more often an external signal generator must be used. It is useful to be able to vary the output voltage of this by known degrees, and an a.m./f.m. modulation facility is useful for most purposes.

Fig. 34. I.C. square wave generator

This integrated circuit square wave generator produces a fast leading edge to the square waveform of roughly 1 kHz, adjustable by changing the value of the 4.7 μF capacitor. The output voltage is 3 V peak-to-peak within a few per cent, and can be taken to a 4.7 kΩ preset potentiometer that has been calibrated by reference to a known oscilloscope waveform to produce an output of 1 V pk-pk.

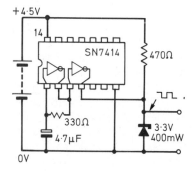

90

Audio signal sources cover the range 20 Hz to 50 kHz, often with extensions at each end of the range. Sine wave outputs are usual with the possible provision of square wave output which allows rapid visual assessment of amplifier frequency response. A special kind of audio oscillator, the function generator, produces low frequency sine, square, triangle, sawtooth and pulse waveforms for analysing specialist circuits with an oscilloscope. The circuit diagram for a simple square wave generator, using a logic integrated circuit, is shown in Fig. 34. The

Fig. 35. Audio amplifier testing

An oscilloscope and square wave generator are useful for testing the response of audio amplifiers. At a frequency of 1 kHz the following effects may be observed, provided that the scope has a good bandwidth of about 1 MHz or more.

(a) Perfection seldom achieved
(b) Slight bass cut
(c) Severe bass cut
(d) Bass boost
(e) Slight treble cut
(f) Severe treble cut
(g) Treble boost
(h) Ringing or parasitic oscillation giving severe distortion or instability

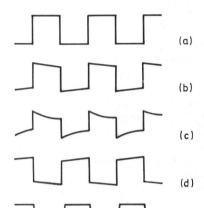

(a)

(b)

(c)

(d)

(e)

(f)

(g)

(h)

effects of different degrees of frequency range limitation are illustrated in Fig. 35. All these waveforms are at the square wave frequency of 1 kHz.

R. F. Signal Generators

An r.f. signal generator takes over where the audio oscillator leaves off, usually 100 kHz, with a frequency range extending to a few tens of

MHz, even higher in some instruments. Above 40 MHz is usually termed v.h.f. and over 400 MHz is u.h.f., although these ranges are usually only provided on expensive instruments.

The output from an r.f. signal generator is a low distortion sine wave. The low distortion means that high order harmonics are not generated which could cause spurious responses in the equipment under test. Often, however, less costly generators allow distortion to occur on the highest frequency range so that harmonics are generated, effectively increasing the range of the instrument, although this effect can give rise to misleading effects when monitoring.

An attenuator is provided so that some adjustment of output amplitude may be made. Accurate attenuation at high frequencies is difficult to achieve (good attenuators can cost several times as much as a modest signal generator) so the controls provided should not be relied upon to provide the basis for any accurate measurements of signal level or gain—the attenuation often varying quite a lot with frequency. The output connection is coaxial to drive 75Ω or 50Ω cable, which should be terminated at the open end with a 75Ω or 50Ω resistor or a 'dummy

Fig. 36. Signal generators

R.F. signal generators have an output impedance of 50 or 75 Ω; the signal must be carried by coaxial cable of matched impedance. The load at the end of the cable should be the same as the cable impedance, otherwise 'reflections' and 'standing waves' will occur, resulting in poor tuning sensitivity.

A dummy aerial can be used to simulate a long wire aerial for receiver tests. One can easily be made up in a diecast box or similar screened metal container from this circuit. The 100 Ω resistor is for a 75 Ω generator (usual). To convert to 50 Ω this resistor should be reduced to 68 Ω.

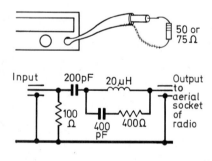

antenna', providing the correct load for the signal generator (Fig. 36). When applied to the aerial socket of a receiver, the receiver will 'think' it has been connected to a matched aerial as it 'sees' the correct source impedance.

92

Signal Injectors

For trouble shooting and general testing a simple signal injector is most useful. A square wave audio oscillator in a hand-held probe generates harmonics up to several hundred MHz which can be injected into

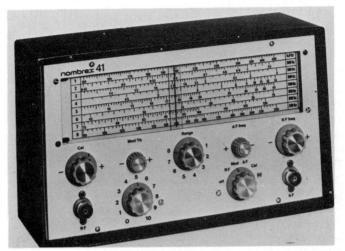

A multi-purpose r.f. signal generator, designed to cover the range 150kHz to 220MHz (courtesy Nombrex (1969) Ltd.)

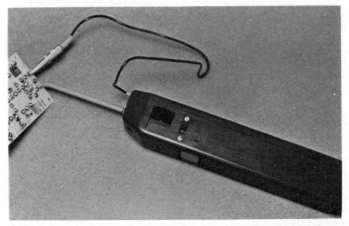

Philips signal injector is typical of many that give an audio output rich in harmonics for fault-finding. This one has a modulated output at 6MHz and 4.43MHz for television servicing

tuners, i.f. amplifiers and audio amplifiers to locate the point at which a signal is 'lost'. They are also useful aids for aligning circuits.

Commercial signal injectors are manufactured by several companies offering useful refinements. Philips make an injector, which, apart from the usual square wave, also gives a modulated r.f. output at 6 MHz (the television sound channel frequency used in the U.K.— elsewhere it may be between 4.4 and 5.5 MHz) and 4.43 MHz (colour subcarrier in U.K.)—very useful for television servicing.

Detectors

To trace a high frequency signal through a circuit, let us say for alignment purposes, an indicator of signal presence is required.

An oscilloscope perhaps gives the most positive indication of the presence of a signal providing it is within the scope's Y amplifier frequency bandwidth. A signal can also be visually discriminated from noise which appears as 'grass' on the oscilloscope screen.

R.F. voltmeters are available which indicate, over a wide frequency range, the voltage present at the probe tip. No discrimination against noise is possible.

The basis of an r.f. voltmeter is simply a rectifying probe followed by a voltmeter, which usually incorporates a transistor amplifier. A simple detector probe can be made up from a few components to drive a conventional voltmeter (Fig. 37), although of course the sensitivity is limited by that of the basic meter.

Fig. 37. R.F. probe

This r,f, detector probe can easily be made up in a cylindrical metal solder dispenser. The probe can be used to feed a d.c. voltmeter, indicating r.f.; an oscilloscope could be used to display modulation envelopes up to a few kilohertz. The carrier frequency range is up to several tens of megahertz, but the maximum input must be limited to 10 V.

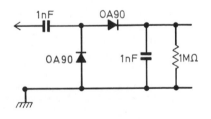

Detector probes are also useful with an oscilloscope as the output is proportional to the applied r.f. and therefore follows the modulation envelope of the signal. The displayed modulation envelope on the scope also shows noise that may be present in the system. Using a detector probe signals well outside the scope's bandwidth can be investigated —the frequency limitations being solely due to the probe.

94

Setting up equipment and finding the faults that are bound to arise during construction is a very logical process and no amount of sophisticated test gear will replace a clear head and a thorough understanding of the circuit operation.

9 Choosing a project

Constructors with some degree of experience will have already learned something about the sort of pitfalls that can be encountered unless consideration is given to the sort of project that it is chosen to undertake. It is so often tempting to go ahead with buying components and starting on the assembly without proper assessment of what one may be letting oneself in for.

Of all the practical projects published in various forms the most popular is usually that which gives an end result that can be used at home. In particular this is true of entertainment equipment, such as radio and hi-fi systems. The beginner is equally likely to think that one can go straight into building anything no matter what the degree of complexity, just so long as one has, or assumes that one has, all the information needed. Tragically, there are many cases when inexperience will tell. Perhaps there is a lack of specialist theoretical knowledge of a particular topic, or maybe there is an assumption that the circuit will operate properly if it is correctly wired according to a circuit diagram. Circuits are intended to be theoretical representations only so that the reader can analyse its working and locate faults if need be.

Before embarking on any project, it is important to consider first if you are confident that when completed it will work properly. If the project is being serialised in a magazine, it is strongly recommended first that you read carefully and study the diagrams given for the first two or three instalments, depending on how much information is given in them. Constructors frequently complain that serialisation involves them in buying more magazines and prolonging the project over several months. However, the most astute will realise that magazines perform other functions within their quota of editorial space to try to provide a reasonably balanced content for a very large readership. Occasionally, long and prestigious projects are reprinted in complete booklet form, incorporating any amendments, and these are a compact way of referring to any part of the project at a later date without scouring the pages of several magazines.

One very important factor in deciding on the choice of project to build will be the estimated cost of the components, including any special materials or tools that you do not have. In Chapter 2, some guidance is given on buying components and a great deal of further information can be obtained from the Constructor's Guide on *Electronic Components*. The prospect of choosing the right components and a suitable supplier may even deter the hesitant constructor from ever starting at all. If you ever find yourself in this situation, it is not a very good plan to rush into buying things you need from the first or obvious supplier suggested. It is possible to gain experience of shopping around by using the telephone; the magazines usually try to help if they can, but do not expect instant results by phone in this case as it can take time to find the answer you require, and the staff invariably have to stop work on the next issue in order to help. If you write to any magazine or component supplier, enclose a stamped self-addressed envelope if you want a reply.

Advertising is the common form of communication to enable you to find how and where to obtain components, but limited space precludes any more than just a short list of selected items. The more comprehensive stockist often produces a catalogue which may include supplementary data on some of the components. These are always worth having for reference. A phone call will establish at the time of ordering if the items you require are in stock.

By studying projects in detail and assessing the supply situation the constructor can determine to some degree what is involved before starting work. Popularity of a particular project can lead to a flood of orders to a handful of suppliers and quickly cause a shortage of stocks in hand. On the other hand there may have been a prior arrangement for the supply of certain items, so one should expect that adequate arrangements are made. Make sure that every item can be obtained before you start or the whole exercise could become aborted. It has been known for well-known or popular items to be specified, only to find that supplies are very limited.

As for the complexity of a project, the actual size of the end result is less significant in many cases than the special constructional techniques required or the critical nature of the layout. You should also make sure that if component substitutes are contemplated, you should be able to do so in non-critical parts of the circuit, or misleading results or even damaged components can be expected. Remembered that once soldered in place, there is little or no chance of compensation if your components are damaged.

Although project details are published in good faith, there is always some element of risk that errors can creep into the printed data. Being human, the designer may even overlook a detail that could have been improved. Later issues sometimes include details of these points and suggest amendments to the project. For this reason it is wise to take your time over construction and assembly in order to be able to incorporate such features as they may come to light later.

There cannot be any hard rules governing the procedure of project selection, because so much depends on the reader's own initiative and assessment. There are established designers whose work appears regularly; by looking back over previous issues one can gain some idea of their work. This does not mean that the reader should ignore newcomers because without these, the authors cannot become established. Of course, much faith has to be placed in the editor who selects the projects felt suitable for publication, but even editors are fallible and often obtain another opinion before deciding on acceptance. In any case the editor is always pleased to hear from readers who have some constructive comment to make on a design, and may even publish a letter that it is felt could help others who are following the project.

In practical project building, the constructor must expect to use initiative and, coupled with a logical approach to any job, can often fill in the gaps of information. It is not reasonable to expect the magazines to publish every single step of construction work because this would occupy an unfair proportion of space. Since they usually cater for a wide range of technical expertise and experience among the readership, only the essential data is likely to be found to satisfy what is considered to be the requirements of the constructor. For this reason, the constructor is advised not to contemplate a project unless everything that is printed is understood. If difficulties are encountered later then advice can be sought from the magazine staff or from someone with experience.

This series of Constructor's Guides has been designed to fill in many of the gaps that magazines cannot allocate space to, except in the occasional supplement. Information on the theory of electronics in all its forms can be obtained from other books and among the leaders in this respect are those published by Newnes-Butterworths, including Beginners Guides and Question and Answers series of books, up to the advanced specialist text books by industrial and educational authors.

Newcomers to radio and electronics are recommended to have a look at these and in conjunction with the Constructor's Guides should have a comprehensive collection of reference books to enable him to tackle constructional projects with confidence. The satisfaction gained from the finished job and the saving in cost is just reward for undertaking what is a unique art and a challenging occupation.

The following is a selection of magazines and journals published in the U.K. that will help the potential electronics constructor.

Everyday Electronics (IPC Magazines Ltd)
Aimed at the newcomer and inexperienced enthusiast interested in fairly straightforward and simple projects. Helps with component choice

Practical Electronics (IPC Magazines Ltd)
Covers a wide range of technical expertise and range of projects for those readers who want state-of-the-art information and challenging projects to build.

Practical Wireless (IPC Magazines Ltd)
Aims to provide a wide selection of projects specially intended for use in the home, with special emphasis on radio and audio subjects.

Wireless World (IPC Electrical-Electronic Press)
Less detailed designs and new ideas in radio and electronic applications, both domestic and industrial.

Electronics Today International
General coverage magazine with features and projects.

Television (IPC Magazines Ltd)
Concentrates on the television side of practical work and includes useful practical projects on test gear.

Radio Control Models & Electronics (Model & Allied Publications Ltd)
Projects allied to models only with associated information.

For the Beginner

Appendix

Tables of useful data for constructors will be found in other volumes of the Constructor's Guides. The following are given as a quick reference.

Table 1. BA Screw threads and drilling sizes

BA	Tapping drills		Clearance drills	
	No.	mm	No.	mm
0	9	5.0	C	6.15
2	24	3.9	12	4.8
4	34	2.8	26	3.75
6	43	2.35	32	3.0
8	50	1.8	43	2.35
10	54	1.4	48	1.95

Table 2. Drill sizes for component wires for p.c.b.s

Wire			Minimum drill size	
s.w.g.	in	mm	No.	mm
10	0.128	3.25	30	3.3
12	0.104	2.64	37	2.65
14	0.080	2.03	46	2.05
16	0.064	1.63	51	1.7
18	0.048	1.22	55	1.3
20	0.036	0.92	60	1.0
≥22	≥0.028	≥0.71	60 to 64	1.0

Table 3. Abbreviations used in this book and elsewhere

A	ampere	mA Milliampere	μA microampere
a.c.	alternating current		
a.f.	audio frequency (up to about 20kHz)		
d.c.	direct current or direct coupled		
DIL	dual-in-line (two rows of pin connections)		
DIN	Deutcher Industrie Normen (German Industrial Standard)		
DPDT	Double-pole double-throw (two-pole, two-way each pole)		
DPST	Double-pole single-throw (two-pole, on-off)		
F	Farad	μF microfarad nF nanofarad	pF picofarad
f.s.d.	Full-scale deflection (of meter)		
H	Henry	mH millihenry	μH microhenry
Hz	Hertz (cycles per second)	kHz kilohertz	MHz megahertz
ht	High tension (main d.c. supply line)		
I	current I_b base current I_c collector current		
	I_e emitter current I_g gate current		
	I_d drain current I_s source current		
	I_f forward current I_r reverse current		
i.c.	integrated circuit		
k	kilo (1,000 times)		
m	milli (one-thousandth)		
μ	micro (one-millionth)		
M	mega (1,000,000 times)		
n	nano (one-thousand-millionth)		
p	pico (one-millionth)		
Ω	ohms	kΩ kilohms	MΩ megohms
p.v.c.	polyvinyl chloride		
p.c.b.	printed circuit board		
r.f.	radio frequency		
SPDT	Single-pole double-throw (one-pole, two way)		
SPST	Single-pole single-throw (one-pole, on-off)		
s.w.g.	Standard Wire Gauge (British)		
V	volts	mV millivolts	μV microvolts
V_{ce}	collector to emitter voltage		
V_{cb}	collector to base voltage		
v.h.f.	very high frequency		
W	watts	mW milliwatts	

Table 4. Standard nominal values or 'preferred' values of resistors with colour codes

Digits and multiples		
0	black	Bye
1	brown	Bye
2	red	Rosie
3	orange	Off
4	yellow	You
5	green	Go
6	blue	Birmingham
7	violet	Via
8	grey	Great
9	white	Western

Sub-multiples

÷1   black (e.g. brown, black, black = 10 ohms)

÷10   gold (e.g. red, red, gold = 2.2 ohms)

÷100 silver (e.g. green, blue, silver = 0.56 ohms)

Digits (1st and 2nd band)		add
10	brown, black	
11	brown, black	
12	brown, red	
15	brown, green	
18	brown, grey	
20	red, black	
22	red, red	
24	red, yellow	
27	red, violet	
30	orange, black	
33	orange, orange	add
36	orange, blue	
39	orange, white	
43	yellow, orange	
47	yellow, violet	
51	green, brown	
56	green, blue	
62	blue, red	
68	blue, grey	
75	violet, green	
82	grey, red	
91	white, brown	

Multiples (3rd band)

÷100	silver
÷10	gold
×1	black
×10	brown
×100	red (kilohms)
×1000	orange
×10,000	yellow
×100,000	green (megohms)
×1,000,000	blue

Tolerance (4th band)

2%	red
5%	gold
10%	silver

103

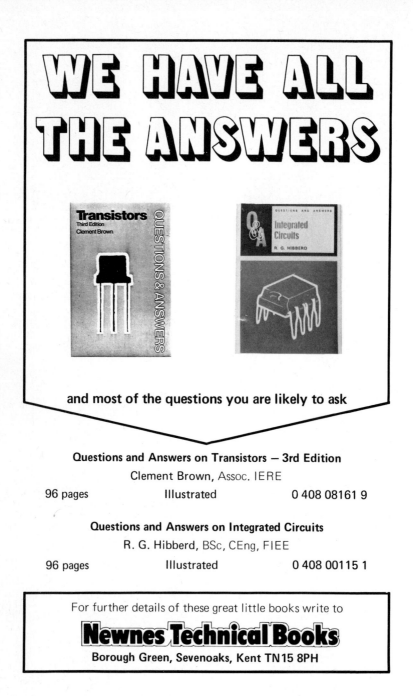

Index

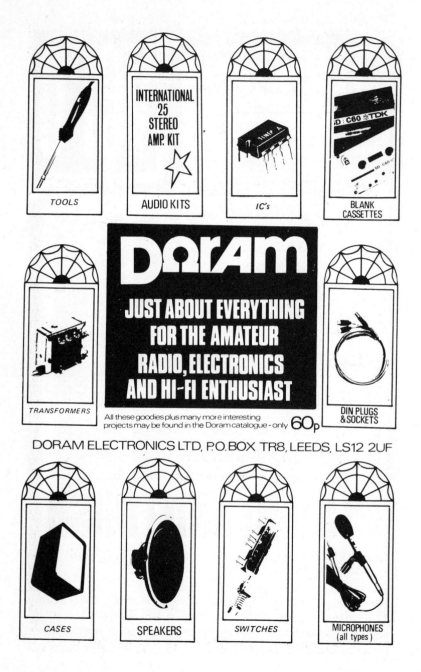

Practical Electronics is the magazine for all home constructors. Every month there is a wide range of useful constructional projects which bring the latest technology within reach of the electronics hobbyist. There are also general features as well as news and comment.

Progress with

PRACTICAL ELECTRONICS

every month 35p.